Marvelous Majolica

An Easy Reference and Price Guide

Jeffrey B. Snyder

Schiffer Publishing Ltd

4880 Lower Valley Road, Atglen, PA 19310 USA

To Jim and Millie Baggs.
To friends separated by distance.
To friends separated by time.
To friends not to be forgotten.
Here's to you, Millie, and to Jim's memory.

Designed by Bonnie M. Hensley
Cover design by Bruce M. Waters
Typeset in Americana XBd BT/ZapfHumanist BT

Printed in China.
ISBN: 0-7643-1275-8
1 2 3 4

Published by Schiffer Publishing Ltd.
4880 Lower Valley Road
Atglen, PA 19310
Phone: (610) 593-1777; Fax: (610) 593-2002
E-mail: Schifferbk@aol.com
Please visit our web site catalog at
www.schifferbooks.com

This book may be purchased from the publisher.
Include $3.95 for shipping. Please try your bookstore first.
We are always looking for people to write books on new and related subjects. If you have an idea for a book please contact us at the above address.
You may write for a free catalog.

In Europe, Schiffer books are distributed by
Bushwood Books
6 Marksbury Avenue
Kew Gardens
Surrey TW9 4JF England
Phone: 44 (0) 20-8392-8585; Fax: 44 (0) 20-8392-9876
E-mail: Bushwd@aol.com
Free postage in the UK. Europe: air mail at cost.

Contents

Acknowledgments

I would like to thank the people who were invaluable to this project, without whom this book would not exist. If it were not so repetitive, every photo caption in this book could end *Courtesy of Michael G. Strawser, Majolica Auctions*. Michael G. Strawser, owner of Majolica Auctions, was instrumental to this project. Mr. Strawser allowed us access to the October 22 and 23, 1999 auction site in Hatfield, Pennsylvania, prior to the auction itself. There we photographed the wares appearing in this book. Among them are majolica wares from the Robert and Mary Good Collection (oyster plates), the estate of Audrey Ottinger, and the Mrs. Ellis E. Stern Collection. If you would like to contact Mr. Strawser about upcoming majolica auctions, he may be reached through the following address: 200 North Main, P.O. Box 332, Wolcottville, Indiana 46795 or through his web site: www.majolicaauctions.com.

To Jennifer Lindbeck and Doug Congdon-Martin, who were with me through a wild night of photography. Their talents enabled us to put together a beautiful book. To Tammy Ward, who input so much data to make the captions possible.

Finally, I would like to thank everyone else who brought this book together in its final form. You know who you are! Thank you, everyone.

Introduction

Ranging from baskets to wall pockets, asparagus holders to wine coolers, majolica wares produced in the latter half of the nineteenth century prove to be endlessly fascinating for collectors. The bright metallic glazes employed by potters in England, Europe, and the United States are dazzling to behold. The shapes and decorations used in the creation of even the most mundane objects are wildly imaginative. Potters made sure their majolica wares kept current with every passing Victorian passion and fancy. As a result, majolica wares were produced featuring decorative motifs and elements from the artistic movements of each passing decade, all the way from Romanticism to Art Nouveau.

Ranging from baskets to wine coolers, majolica wares prove endlessly fascinating. A very rare handled wicker basket by Griffen, Smith & Company of Phoenixville, Pennsylvania. 7.75" w. x 6" h. $1200+

This book is intended to provide readers with a quick reference guide to the startling and diverse world of majolica ceramics. The text provides an overview of majolica itself and the pottery firms that produced it in England, Europe, and the United States. The majolica wares themselves are organized under two general, and hopefully self-explanatory, headings: "Around the House" and "For the Table & for Tea." Under these general headings, wares are organized alphabetically by type. It is hoped that this approach will provide the reader with a quick identification and values guide useful in the field, at auction, and at home. For more in-depth studies of majolica wares and the potters who produced them, a variety of excellent sources are listed as well under Recommended Readings.

This cobalt swan wine cooler with cattails by Minton is outstanding in color and detail. It dates to 1868. Beginning in 1842, Minton's firm began using "year ciphers" on their wares, with an individual cipher (symbol) indicating a specific potting year for those who can read them. These are usually accompanied by an impressed capital letter code indicating the month the ware it appears on was produced. With these, it is a fairly simple matter to date Minton's wares. (For a complete listing of the year ciphers and month codes, see Kowalsky 1999, p. 289.) 11" h. x 10" d. $5500+

What is Majolica?

The ceramic body of majolica is a low fired, soft earthenware. After an initial firing to harden the clay body into "bisque," the porous bisque must be covered with glaze to render it impervious to water. In the case of majolica, an opaque glaze or slip initially coated the bisque. Once that opaque coat was dried (but prior to the glaze firing), it was painted with vibrant metallic oxide glazes that gave majolica its brilliant coloration. Those who applied these metallic oxides had to take care, as the color changed once it was fired. Copper produced green, manganese provided a brownish-purple, cobalt a deep blue, and so on.

Often, majolica wares were molded with either low or high relief designs prior to the bisque firing. In certain cases, these designs created "figural"

Majolica is a soft bodied earthenware decorated with vibrant metallic oxide glazes that give it the startling colors that first attract the eye. Often majolica wares are molded in fanciful forms that hold attention once they have captured that attention with the glazes. Mottled triple dolphin footed bowl by Wedgwood. 4" h. $250-275

wares. To be considered a majolica figural, a piece should feature a high relief, three-dimensional figure that constitutes or encompasses between sixty and seventy-five percent of the item. This percentage is, in certain cases, quite flexible. If the figure is considered the focal point of the majolica object, that figure may involve as

"Vintagers" pattern figural centerpiece (featuring two grape harvesters, shape number 728, marked with the year cipher 1867) produced by Minton. Missing from this piece is a center bowl supported by the rods the harvesters hold. In a line drawing of the pattern found in Minton majolica rag books, the bowl is roughly rectangular in shape and would have been modeled with a basketweave pattern and a scalloped edge. (To examine the Minton pattern drawing, see Dawes 1990, p. 54.) 16" h. x 19" l. This extraordinary centerpiece sold for $2250 at auction and could easily bring in excess of $4000 on the secondary market. A modified version of the leading figure as a single figure carrying a basket in his arms and another on his back was offered by present-day dealers for $2000.

little as fifty percent of the piece. A wide variety of mythical creatures, animals, and humans all cavort across majolica's figurals.

Here are a pair of Minton figural spill vases depicting a boy and a girl leaning on baskets that contained the spills. (See the "Spill Vases" section for an explanation of their use.) $3000+ pair

A Minton trident armed putti rests atop a nautilus shell. This fine example of Minton's figural work is shape number 1885 and dates from 1882. 17" h. This magnificent figure brought $5250 at auction.

The term "majolica" itself is a trade name developed by the Staffordshire potter, Herbert Minton (who, working with a talented staff, created the ware), to identify this distinctive ceramic form when it was introduced in England around 1850. In its earliest incarnation, English majolica was patterned after Italian tin glazed earthenware known as maiolica; maiolica was an Italian term identifying luster ware from Valencia, which had been shipped in the sixteenth century from the island of Maiolica, now Majorca. This Renaissance ware was being written about by scholars in the mid-nineteenth century, acquired by museums, purchased by wealthy antiquarians for their private collections, and coveted by many more. To be able to purchase wares looking much like the desirable maiolica antiquities for prices the then rising middle class could afford was quite alluring.

The term "Toby" is applied to jugs (a.k.a. pitchers) modeled in the likeness of the entire human form, head to toe.
This toby jug (pitcher) features a drunken army reservist straddling the barrel. It was produced by the French firm Frie Onnaing and is considered scarce. 11" h. $470-515

In contrast, "character" jugs refer to items molded in the likeness of only the human head or head and shoulders.
Left: "Puck" character (or face) jug by the French firm Sarreguemines. It is shape number 652 and measures 7.5" h. $275-350
Right: Sarreguemines "Puck" character jug, shape number 653. $275-350

Minton's majolica was very successful. Other English potters quickly introduced majolica wares of their own. Soon the Europeans would follow, producing majolica in both the English style and in more Continental motifs. In time, American potters would enter this colorful market as well. The vast majority of American majolica was more practical in nature than that produced by either English or Continental potters, providing far more bread trays and butter pats than garden seats and vases.

Majolica wares would be produced from roughly 1850 on into the first quarter of the twentieth century. Majolica's peak production years would fall between 1850 and 1890. Once the middle class had purchased all the majolica they cared to own, potters who manufactured majolica on into the first quarter of the twentieth century had to market their wares elsewhere. These later items were primarily lower quality, inexpensive majolica wares offered as fair prizes, premiums, promotions, and souvenirs for the tourist trade.

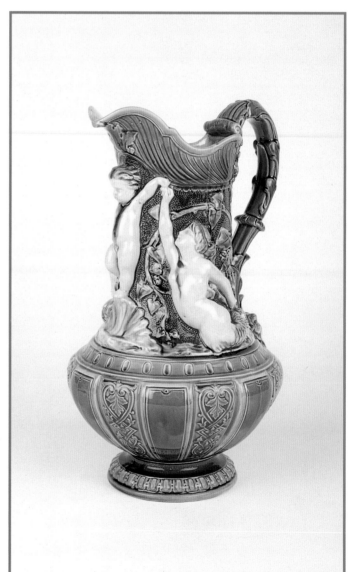

Minton's majolica was quite popular. Minton mermaid pitcher with periwinkle blue rim and panels measuring 12" high. This pitcher is shape number 474 and is dated by its year cipher to 1863. This piece sold at auction for $2750. It would not be surprising to see it command $4000+ in mint condition on the secondary market.

This is a Minton "Satyr" wall bracket shelf. The satyr blows a horn and carries a fox slung over the shoulder. A gray fur keeps the mythical creature decent while green and yellow oak leaves and acorns hang over its head. This highly detailed piece dates from 1867 and measures 18.5" high. It is one of a pair displayed later in this book. (For additional wall bracket shelves, see Snyder et al. 1994, p. 61.) Together at auction, these wall bracket shelves sold for $16,000!

Other English potters quickly introduced majolica wares of their own. This unusual footed salt cellar featuring three lambs' heads, swags, and cobalt accents was produced by Wedgwood. The pattern was registered with the British patent office on September 22, 1864. $340+

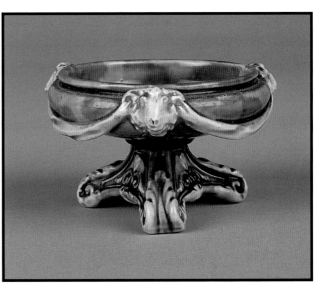

Soon the Europeans would follow, producing majolica in both the English style and in more Continental motifs. This Sarreguemines monkey pitcher measures 9.5" high. $450-495

American potters would enter this colorful market as well. This sunflower pitcher was produced by the prolific American firm Griffen, Smith & Company of Phoenixville, Pennsylvania. 6.5" h. $265+

Who Manufactured Majolica?

What follows is a brief review of the major majolica manufacturers in England, on the Continent, and in the United States. When dates are presented in parentheses, along with the general locations of the potting factories discussed, these dates indicate the years each firm was in business, not the dates for each firm's majolica production. As with all things historical, as further research is conducted, these dates may well be subject to revision when new information comes to light.

In England

Herbert Minton's Minton Porcelain Manufacturing Company (Stoke-on-Trent, Staffordshire, 1793-present) profited from the Paris Revolution of 1848. The worker's revolt sent many artisans fleeing France for England's shores. Minton hired Léon Arnoux at this time, a talented French potter destined to become Minton's art director. Arnoux in turn added several other accomplished French artisans to the mix. Together with the company's principle designer, Thomas Kirby, the convergence of English and French techniques and design produced the first majolica wares. While the earliest wares to bear the trade name majolica appear in Minton's pattern books in 1849, the general public was made aware of majolica at the Crystal Palace Exhibition (what many have termed the "First World's Fair") in London in 1851.

Following the success of the Crystal Palace Exhibition, Minton maintained a touring stock of impressive majolica items guaranteed to peak the interest of consumers and competitors alike. With his touring stock, Minton's firm maintained a presence at international exhibitions throughout the 1850s and well on into the following decades. This presence served the firm well, generating interest at home and abroad in these brightly colored and creatively designed wares. By the time of Herbert Minton's death in 1858, the company was recognized as one of the largest decorative ceramic manufacturers in the western world.

Minton's fanciful teapot, featuring a monkey with cobalt jacket holding coconut, is dated by the year cipher (a.k.a. date code) to 1865. 8" l. x 6.5" h. $4200-4600

There is a lot to be learned from a Minton manufacturer's mark. This is a typical impressed MINTONS mark. This mark was in use from 1873 to 1951. (Prior to that, the impressed MINTON mark without the S was used for a about a decade from c.1862-1872.) A year cipher (the triangle within the circle to the right of the MINTONS mark) for the years 1876 accompanies the manufacturer's mark. An impressed A month letter indicates the piece (an oyster plate to be seen later) was produced in April. (Minton's single letter month codes are: J-January; F-February; M-March; A-April; E-May; I-June; H-July; Y-August; S-September; O-October; N-November; and D-December.) To the lower left is the diamond shaped registration mark, indicating the original date of registration with the British patent office to be January 3, 1868.

To properly read these diamond shaped registration marks you need to know that from 1842 to 1867 the year letter code appears at the apex of the diamond beneath the circle that includes the Roman numeral IV—the code for ceramics. The letter code for the month appears on the left side of the diamond and the day of the month in Arabic numerals appears to the right. From 1868 to 1883, the locations were changed. The year letter code appears on the right, the day of the month at the appex, and the month letter code at the base. The **month code** is as follows and remains the same throughout: C-January; G-February; W-March; H-April; E-May; M-June; I-July; R-August; D-September; B-October; K-November; and A-December. From **1842-1867**, the **year codes** are: X-1842; H-1843; C-1844; A-1845; I-1846; F-1847; U-1848; S-1849; V-1850; P-1851; D-1852; Y-1853; J-1854; E-1855; L-1856; K-1857; B-1858; M-1859; Z-1860; R-1861; O-1862; G-1863; N-1864; W-1865; Q-1866; and T-1867. From **1868-1883**, the **year codes** are: X-1868; H-1869; C-1870; A-1871; I-1872; F-1873; U-1874; S-1875; V-1876; P-1877; D-1878; Y-1879; J-1880; E-1881; L-1882; and K-1883. After 1883, the informative diamond marks were replaced by simpler, yet less illuminating, registration numbers listed as Rd followed by a number. These registration numbers simply ascend consecutively, beginning with number 1 in 1884.

Please note the two white unglazed spots that appear on the base (to the right and above the impressed 3). These are stilt marks left by (often three legged) stilts that support the wares when they are fired, raising the glaze above the surface of a "sagger" (a clay vessel that protects the objects being fired in the kiln) so that the glaze will not adhere to the sagger itself. When the fired piece is removed from the kiln, the stilts are snapped off, leaving behind these marks. These should not be considered damage but merely common artifacts of the firing process.

The venerable Wedgwood and Company pottery firm, established in the mid-eighteenth century (Staffordshire, c. 1759-present), entered the majolica market in 1862. As Wedgwood hired a number of Minton's designers and modelers to produce majolica on a freelance basis, many of Wedgwood's early majolica offerings are quite similar to Minton's. By 1880, the Wedgwood designs diverged from Minton's. At that time, the prolific firm was offering over 350 majolica pottery pieces to the general public. Tablewares were their specialties; the firm was almost unrivaled in their production of useful majolica wares for the table and around the house. So admired were Wedgwood's majolica offerings in Europe that many Continental potters frequently imitated Wedgwood's designs.

A pair of figures, a young woman with a serpent and a winged boy with a quiver of arrows (Cupid?)—a dangerous combination to be sure, by Wedgwood. 8" h. each. This pair sold at auction for $1250.

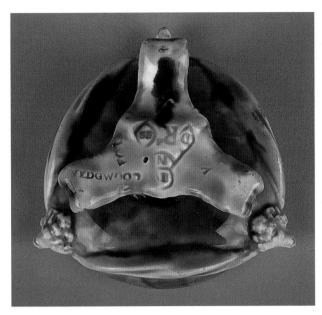

The 1870s proved to be a peak period of majolica production for Wedgwood. Japanese designs became popular during this period, and Wedgwood produced a formal, sparcely decorated majolica ware christened "Argenta" to meet the public's demand for Japanese decorative motifs. Argenta featured limited, colorfully glazed molded relief decoration that contrasted well with the off-white body. Wedgwood continued to manufacture majolica on into the twentieth century, in greatly reduced quantities that reflected the sharp drop in demand.

An impressed WEDGWOOD mark accompanied by a registration mark indicating the registry date to be September 22, 1864. Wedgwood used a three letter code to indicate the month, potter, and year of production. A partial three letter code may be seen just above the Wedgwood manufacturer's mark. (See Kowalsky 1999, p. 368 for a complete interpretation of Wedgwood's three letter code.)

The talented potter George Jones apprenticed with Minton in the 1850s. It is therefore no particular surprise that upon the establishment of his George Jones & Sons Ltd. pottery factory (Stoke-on -Trent, Staffordshire, 1861-1907), Jones soon rivaled Minton in the production of quality majolica wares. George Jones focused on the production of useful, rather than ornamental, wares, including ashtrays, footed centerpieces, cheese domes, caviar servers, oyster plates, sardine boxes, place card stands, and spittoons.

Among George Jones & Sons' more popular patterns were "Dogwood," "Dogwood and Woven Fence," and "Iris and Lily." The firm also became well known for the use of English birds as decorative motifs, and for their proclivity to produce humorous pieces from time to time. As demand for majolica declined in England in the 1880s, however, George Jones & Sons largely turned to the production of other wares.

This basket tureen, featuring a fish atop a bed of leaves and ferns on the lid, was produced by George Jones. 15.25" l. $4600+

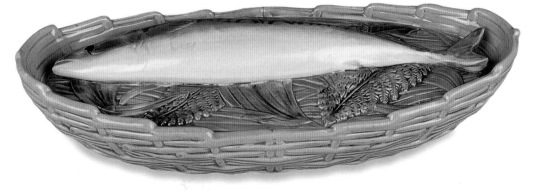

One common characteristic of much of George Jones' majolica is the glazing of the bases of his wares with a distinctive green and brown tortoiseshell pattern. It is interesting to note that possibly the largest American majolica producer, Griffen, Smith & Company, also decorated the bases of some of their majolica wares with a tortoiseshell motif.

Other well known English pottery firms producing majolica included Brown-Westhead, Moore & Company (Shelton, Hanley, Staffordshire, c. 1862-1904), W.T. Copeland & Sons (Stoke-on-Trent, Staffordshire, 1847-1970), Simon Fielding & Company (Stoke, Staffordshire, 1879 onward), and Joseph Holdcroft (Longton, Staffordshire, 1865-1939).

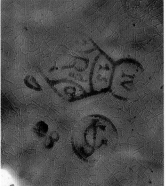

This George Jones manufacturer's mark is a simple GJ monogram in a circle. It dates from roughly 1861 to 1873. In 1873, the firm would add "& SONS" to the mark. A partial registration mark is also visible.

On the Continent

Prior to the introduction of Minton's majolica, Charles Jean Avisseau (b. 1796-d. 1861), a potter in Tours, France, began creating pottery that successfully reproduced the elaborate earthenwares made during the Renaissance by the talented Frenchman Bernard Palissy. Avisseau's wares, first potted in 1829, were handmade. They featured intricate detailing and elegant figures of sea creatures, reptiles, and insects that were true to the style of Palissy's sixteenth century master works.

Avisseau's efforts inspired other French potters to follow in his footsteps, creating all manner of imaginative, decorative wares in the Palissy style. In 1855, Avisseau, joined by his son and daughter, displayed his wares at the Paris Exhibition. The wide recognition and praise the Avisseaus received quickly translated into a demand for Palissy-style wares, particularly in France.

After Charles Avisseau's death, other manufacturers created Palissy wares in more contemporary styles to broaden the market base. While French manufacturers continued to produce Palissy ware, the primary manufacturers of later wares in the Palissy style would be Portuguese potters from Caldas da Rainha, Portugal.

Today, many choose to include Palissy wares under majolica's banner. However, while the glazing is colorful and the surface decorations are intricate indeed, the methods of manufacture differ significantly and, of course, Palissy ware's origins well precede majolica's. It is not hard, in fact, to see how a manufacturer of the intricate Palissy-style ware could easily transition into creating the less technically demanding majolica ceramics. Indeed, some potters applied Palissy decorative motifs to majolica wares, using majolica's mass-production manufacturing techniques, blurring the lines between the ware types and adding to present-day collectors' difficulties.

Following the Paris and London Exhibitions of 1855 and 1862, European potters from France, Germany, Austria, Central Europe, the Scandinavian countries and Portugal all began producing majolica. Some European potters produced majolica in the English style while others turned to their own Rennaissance antiquities (as Avisseau had done) for inspiration and design. The potteries in France, Germany, and Austria were the most likely to produce majolica based on English designs, with the largest quantities emanating from the Sarreguemines factory in Lorraine, France.

This round plaque displays the Portuguese interpretation of Palissy ware, featuring a snake, a frog, a lizard, and insects on a bed of grass, and is signed José A. Cunha. 7"d. $1200+

A monumental French Palissy ware cobalt platter, signed on the front "RDE Blois," and on the back "F.B.D. 1897, #7811." This startling platter is encrusted with molded sea creatures, shells, and seaweed. 15" l. $3600+

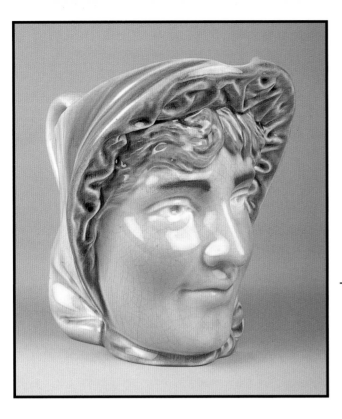

In France

Sarreguemines, established in Lorraine in 1770, began producing majolica after the 1862 exhibition. This firm, the largest in France, brought forth majolica wares rivaling those of Minton. Included among Sarreguemines' majolica offerings were ornamental, figural, and novelty items, architectural forms, and useful wares with a heavy emphasis on dessert services. Sarreguemines majolica tended to be heavy and long lasting. The company would produce high quality majolica wares on into the early twentieth century.

This Sarreguemines bonnet wearing "Danish Woman" character jug measures 7" high and is shape number 3319. $500-700

A typical impressed SARREGUEMINES manufacturer's mark appears on the base of the Danish Woman character jug. Additionally, from 1898 to 1905, Sarreguemines conveniently added the month and year of production to their jugs. In the photo, the number 3319 is the model number, 03 represents the year of production (1903), the letter C indicates the decorator, the number 1 represents either the month of production (January) or the size of the piece, and the 27 is part of the number 227 indicating the piece is majolica. (For additional information on Sarreguemines' marks and the firm's wares, see Cunningham 1997, pp. 51-76.)

Choisy-le-Roi (Choisy-le-Roi, France) was established as a faïence pottery in 1804. In the early 1860s, like Sarreguemines, Choisy-le-Roi added majolica to their production and would continue manufacturing majolica wares until 1910. While a fascination with Renaissance wares had a strong influence on majolica design in the early 1860s, the introduction of Japanese decorative motifs at the Paris exhibitions of 1867 and 1878 strongly influenced the artists at Choisy. Assymetrical Oriental motifs dominated Choisy designs during this period. Other decorative motifs employed by the firm during the last quarter of the nineteenth century included a variation on shell-and-seaweed patterns and leaf plates.

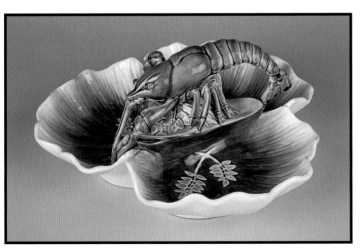

This Choisy-le-Roi lobster three part server measures 13" wide. $325-360

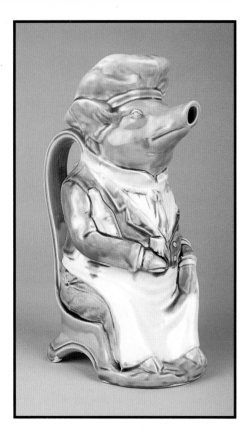

La Faïencerie d'Onnaing of northern France produced lower quality majolica in large quantities. Theirs were largely examples of the later inexpensive majolica wares produced for the novelty export market. Onnaing majolica was made from 1870 to 1900 and is generally characterized by muddy glaze colors applied with no particular attention to detail. Among their majolica wares were candlestick holders, children's toys, small clocks, flowerpots, vases, umbrella stands, smoking accessories, and dinnerwares. Their tobacco jars, match strikers, and ashtrays were molded in a variety of whimsical forms including bears, devils, dragons, frogs, and vultures.

This whimsical pig waiter pitcher was produced by Onnaing and measures 10.5" high. $475-575

Typical Onnaing manufacturer's mark.

Other notable French majolica manufacturers included Keller et Guerin, Luneville, and Saint Clément.

In Central Europe, Germany, and Scandinavia

Three firms from Bohemia are known for their majolica production: Wilhelm Schiller and Son, Julius Dressler, and B. Bloch and Company. Of the three, Wilhelm Schiller and Son was the most prolific. Established in 1829 (then Schiller and Gerbing—the Wilhelm Schiller and Son name would not be adopted until 1885), Schiller began producing majolica wares in the 1860s. The company's majolica was well modeled and featured glaze color combinations characteristic of Central Europe. D. Michael Murray aptly described Bohemian majolica glazes such as Schiller's as having the appearance of a "varnished finish." (Murray 1997, 7)

St. Clément rooster pitcher, 13" h. $350-515

Schiller specialized in decorative majolica, including some very impressive ornamental vases, centerpieces, ewers, jardinieres and pedestals, wall plaques, and wall pockets. However, the firm also produced many more practical wares destined for more frequent use, including candlesticks, card trays, humidors, lamps, matchboxes, pitchers, and steins.

As the First World War loomed over Europe, Wilhelm Schiller and Son ceased production and closed the factory.

Wilhelm Schiller and Son scenic monk tobacco jar. $175-195

Julius Dressler established his pottery dedicated to the manufacture of majolica and porcelain at about the same time as the Schiller firm launched their majolica lines (1860s). Dressler's company produced decorative serving wares including asparagus and berry sets, along with egg platters. Dressler would cease majolica production around 1910, although the firm would continue to produce pottery until 1945.

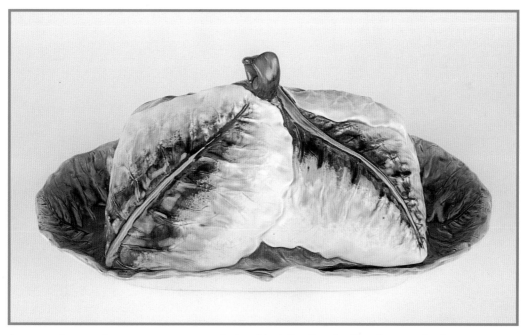

An unusual covered asparagus server manufactured by Julius Dressler. Dressler was a leader among Central European potters in the manufacture of both asparagus and berry servers. Two marks appear on Dressler's majolica: the first features the initials JDB (for Julius Dressler, Biela [the site of the factory]) encompassed by a tower or possibly a kiln stack; the later mark features a circle of stars surrounding a standing griffen and the stylized initials DB. (To view Dressler's marks, see Murray 1997, p. 57.) This server brought $625 at auction.

In 1871, B. Bloch and Company was founded, in part for the production of majolica. The firm was one of the few that would continue producing majolica on into the 1930s. Bloch and Company's early majolica wares included smoking accessories for pipes and cigars. Among them were elaborate smoker's companions, which combined a cigar holder, match holder, striker, and occasionally a receptacle for burnt matches.

B. Bloch and Company also produced extravagant ewers and centerpieces for which they became well known. Figural animal bottles were also among the company's repertoire. Heading into the twentieth century, the firm dropped much of the Victorian ornamentation and produced largely useful and inexpensive majolica wares, including bowls, baskets, cachepots, and sconces.

In Hungary, Miklos Zsolnay established a pottery in the 1850s. In 1868, the Zsolnay factory turned to the production of quality, decorative majolica wares, including ewers, garden seats, teapots, and vases. Zsolnay would continue to produce elegant majolica wares until 1900.

This smoke set displays a sinister fox overpowering his victim, a sheep. Produced by B. Bloch and Company and simply marked with a "BB" monogram. $425-465

The largest German majolica manufacturer was Villeroy and Boch (Mettlach and other European locations, 1836-present). From roughly the 1850s to 1900, the firm generated prodigious quantities of majolica, including leaf plates and other tablewares reminiscent of English designs. This was a wise choice, as much of Villeroy and Boch's majolica was destined for American shores where the bias was toward "all pottery English!" After 1900, the firm created a souvenir majolica line.

Georg Schneider was another notable German majolica manufacturer, producing majolica wares from c. 1890 to 1920. The company created both useful majolica lines in the English style and majolica souvenir items. Most common among their majolica wares were dessert plates. Ornamental majolica was left to other firms.

Most of the majolica emanating from Scandinavia was produced by the Arabia Pottery, founded outside Helsinki, Finland, in 1874. A subsidiary company to Rörstrand Pottery of Sweden, Arabia produced large and functional majolica plant stands and jardinieres in the Art Nouveau style.

This Villeroy and Boch rabbit charger measures 12" in diameter. This charger sold at auction for $500.

This VBS (Villeroy & Boch Schramberg) mark was in use from roughly 1883-1912 on majolica wares. If the item bearing this mark had been sent to the United States (as is likely) then Made In Germany would have been added from 1891 onward in accordance with the McKinley act, which basically insisted that imports must be identified as such by labeling them with their country of origins.

In Portugal

Portuguese pottery firms producing majolica and Palissy-style wares included José A. Cunha, Mafra and Son, The Manufacture Royale de Rato, and Rafael Bordalo Pinheiro. With the exception of The Manufacture Royale de Rato (Lisbon), all were located in Caldas da Rainha. Of these firms, Mafra and Son produced the vast majority of the Palissy-style wares emanating from Portugal (beginning in 1853) while José A. Cunha was well known around 1900 for majolica tablewares in imaginatively designed leaf forms. The Manufacture Royale de Rato was both a significant manufacturer of majolica and an exhibitor of Palissy-style ware in the Paris Exhibition of 1867. Rafael Bordalo Pinheiro (1883 onward) manufactured a diverse range of majolica tiles, examples of which were on display at the Paris Exhibition of 1889.

Oval José A. Cunha manufacturer's mark including the location of the factory (Caldas Rainha) and the country of origin.

This José A. Cunha Palissy ware plaque features lizards and a frog. 9.5" dia. $1200+

An impressed M. MAFRA CALDAS PORTUGAL manufacturer's mark with a crown.

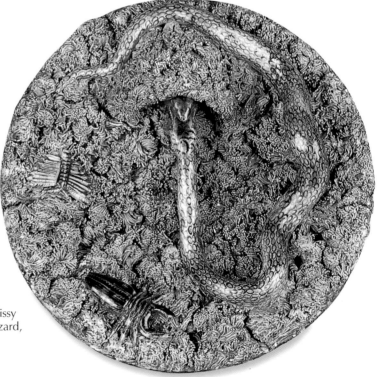

An equally elaborate M. Mafra Caldas Palissy ware plaque is adorned with a serpent, lizard, and beetles. 8" dia. $1000+

In the United States

For centuries, American potters had been unable to compete against the long established potteries of England. Over time, a bias developed among American consumers: they believed that English pottery was far superior to anything an upstart American potter could create. The struggling American artisans felt that the Centennial Exhibition of 1876 in Philadelphia, Pennsylvania, offered them their best chance to change the minds of America's consumers. Some potters, Edwin Bennett, James Carr, and J. E. Jeffords among them, felt that majolica was the proper ware to show off American potting prowess. Americans in the thousands saw the "home-grown" majolica and were impressed. The Centennial Exhibition did for majolica potters in the United States what the Crystal Palace Exhibition had done for Herbert Minton a quarter century earlier. As a result, the decade of the 1880s would see high demand for majolica wares in the United States. In fact, the 1880s would be a most colorful decade. Along with majolica, advances in lithography were creating color advertising and packaging found to be most impressive by American consumers.

Immigrant British potters William and Edwin Bennett established the E. & W. Bennett pottery in Baltimore, Maryland, in 1848. William left the firm in 1856 and the name changed to the Edwin Bennett Pottery. Having displayed his majolica during the Centennial Exhibition, Bennett would go on to produce majolica wares during the 1880s, when demand for majolica in America was at its height. The Bennett factory was the largest pottery firm in the Baltimore area and remained active until c. 1937.

James Carr arrived in the United States from England in 1844. He had worked with well-known British potters James Clews and John Ridgway prior to his arrival. By 1853, Carr had established his own pottery works, the New York City Pottery, in Manhattan. In the years to come, Carr would train many American potters who would go on to successfully produce majolica, including J. E. Jeffords.

Majolica wares were added to Carr's high quality product line in the mid-1860s. Included among his majolica offerings was a combination of the useful and the ornamental, including centerpieces, compotes, game dishes, garden seats, match strikers, pitchers, sardine boxes, and vases. Best known among Carr's majolica was a line decorated in a cauliflower motif similar to a Wedgwood design. It is not surprising, in fact, that English designs and techniques were often used in the creation of Carr's majolica.

Majolica from The New York City Pottery won awards at both the Centennial Exhibition and the Paris Exposition of 1878. Carr's firm would continue to produce majolica wares until 1888, when the factory closed.

Once trained by James Carr, J. E. Jeffords founded his Philadelphia City Pottery in 1868. Jeffords was well known for casting unusually large pottery. The public's attention was quickly captured by his twenty gallon teapot, complete with a four foot high majolica pedestal, featured at the Centennial Exhibition. Jeffords' Philadelphia City Pottery would continue producing majolica and other wares until the factory ceased production in 1890.

While Griffen, Smith & Company, originally Griffen, Smith and Hill, may not have been among the first American potteries to produce majolica, many ceramics historians have considered the firm one of the best and most prolific. Established in an existing pottery factory in Phoenixville, Pennsylvania, in 1879 by American brothers Henry and George Griffen and English potter, David Smith, the firm began producing majolica in 1882.

Having missed the Centennial Exhibition in Philadephia, Griffen, Smith & Company took advantage of the World's Industrial and Cotton Centennial Exposition in New Orleans in 1884. Here they won critical acclaim and, with the help of a colorful catalog of their majolica wares printed for the occasion, captured the attention of the American public.

Struggling American artisans felt that the Centennial Exhibition of 1876 in Philadelphia, Pennsylvania, offered them their best chance to convince American consumers that they could indeed compete with the English potters, producing wares of both high quality and reasonable price. A Centennial Philadelphia umbrella stand with the Liberty Bell and Independence Hall molded in relief. 22" high. $300+

The vast majority of the majolica wares produced by this prolific firm were useful in nature, including bowls, butter pats, compotes, covered dishes, plates, platters, tea sets, and tobacco jars. Wide ranging decorative motifs were employed. Like Choisy-le-Roi in France, shell-and-seaweed, leaf patterns (a single Begonia leaf design used for pickle dishes and pin trays was popular), and Japanese assymetrical motifs (most often including either birds or bamboo in the decoration) were employed to good effect. Also produced were wares featuring sunflowers, vegetables, additional foliage of all sorts, and a variety of popular British motifs (including "Albino" majolica featuring a Japanese-style motif—basically a white background glaze adorned with minimal molded and colored glazed border decoration similar to Wedgwood's Argenta). The previously mentioned bamboo motif was a favorite with many American majolica manufacturers in the 1880s. Griffen, Smith & Company produced a wide selection of bamboo adorned bowls, cream pitchers, sugar bowls, teapots, and spooners.

In 1889, David Smith was forced to retire in poor health. His shares in the business were sold to J. Stuart Love, Henry Griffen's father-in-law. The company name changed to Griffen, Love & Company. This sale curtailed any further serious majolica production in Phoenixville. In the winter of 1890, with interest in majolica on the decline in the United States, a massive fire nearly destroyed the factory. While a number of lesser operators would use the site and continue to produce small amounts of majolica until c. 1902, the firm never truly recovered from the disastrous blaze.

It is pleasant to note, however, just how hard it can be to keep a good man down. As the nineteenth century drew to a close, David Smith came out of retirement to assist a small, short-lived Pennsylanvania potting firm, the Chester County Pottery Company. Smith began his association by designing commemorative wares for the presidential campaign of 1896.

A large shell-and-seaweed pattern teapot with a crooked spout produced by Griffen, Smith & Company. 6.5" high. $1000-1400

A shell-and-seaweed pattern 6" high pitcher by Griffen, Smith & Company. $845-930

Begonia leaf butter pat by Griffen, Smith & Company, measuring 3.75" in diameter. $275+

A cauliflower teapot by Griffen, Smith & Company. 5.75" h. $1230-1350

Griffen, Smith & Company's GSH monogram mark surrounded by twin circles including the words ETRUSCAN MAJOLICA. The M5 code refers to the company's letter designation for vessel form (in this case M was used for bowls, covered jars, bonbon dishes, and some plates) and number designation for style of decoration. The letter code designations are as follows: A-individual butter plates, round, leaf or flower shape; B-pickle dishes, usually in irregular leaf shape; C-cake trays or dishes, leaf or flower shape with irregular or round shape; D-plates in varying patterns, round with conventional leaf or shell shape; E-hollow forms, pitchers, coffee/teapots, syrup jugs, sugar and slop bowls; F-cuspidors, jardinieres; G-cake baskets; H-bonbon dishes, in deep oval form; I-covered boxes; J-comports with pedestals or stands; K-paper weights, pin trays, small flower jars, special forms of cheese dishes and trays; L-celery vases, mugs, shakers, jewel trays and comports with dolphin-shaped feet; M-bowls, covered jars, bonbon dishes, and certain plates; N-covered cheese and sardine boxes; and O-cups and saucers. This M5 mark was found on the base of a shell-and-seaweed pattern decorated nappy bowl. Collectors and dealers alike often refer to the majolica of Griffen, Smith & Company simply as "Etruscan."

At the time Griffin, Smith and Company was producing majolica, there was significant public interest in Etrusan revivalist decorative arts. The firm promptly christened their majolica "Etruscan." The name harkened back to the potters of ancient Rome in the last seven centuries B.C., grounding the company's increasingly popular modern ware in the romance of the works of centuries past. Minton had done just the same thing a quarter century before them.

Many other American potteries, both large and small, took to the production of majolica during the height of its popularity. Among their ranks were Arsenal Pottery (Trenton, New Jersey), The Chesapeake Pottery Company (Baltimore, Maryland), Eureka Pottery (Trenton, New Jersey), The Faience Manufacturing Company (Greenpoint, New York), The Hampshire Pottery (Keene, New Hampshire), Morley & Company (Wellsville and East Liverpool, Ohio), The New Milford Pottery Company (later the Wannopee Pottery Company, New Milford, Connecticut), Odell and Booth Brothers (Tarrytown, New York), Peekskill Pottery Company (Peekskill, New York), and Willets Manufacturing Company (Trenton, New Jersey).

A vibrant cobalt glazed background makes the bird in flight pattern stand out on this double handle vase by Eureka Pottery Co. (Trenton, New Jersey, 1883-1887). 9.5" h. $900+

A Word About Pricing

The prices found in the captions are in United States dollars. Prices vary immensely based on the location of the market, the venue of the sale, and the enthusiasms of the collecting community. Prices in the Midwest differ from those in the West or East, and those at specialty shows or auctions will differ from those in dealer's shops or through dealer's web pages.

All of these factors make it impossible to create absolutely accurate price listings, but a guide to realistic pricing may be offered. In the cases of rare and unusual items that do not often appear on the secondary market and, therefore, do not have a reliable, established secondary market value (or for items that had prices which seemed dubious at best), I have provided the prices brought at auction for such items and have clearly marked them as auction values. **Please note:** these values are not provided to set prices in the antiques marketplace, but rather to give the reader a reasonable idea of what one might expect to pay for mint condition majolica.

Baskets

Continental

An unusual Continental basket featuring a baby with wings balanced on its rim. 11" h. $225+

Unattributed

Collectors soon discover that many majolica items were left unmarked and are now very difficult—if not impossible—to identify by manufacturer. There are a number of reasons why this is the case. For example, small firms with little or no name recognition with the buying public were unlikely to go to the extra effort and expense of creating a manufacturer's mark for, and including it on, their wares when it would have no positive influence over a buyer's decision. This is particularly true of small firms that patterned their wares after popular lines of larger, respected firms. For them, if a customer should think their product to be that of a well known manufacturer, so much the better! Even the largest firms did not always mark every piece. If items were sold together as part of a set, there was no need for the potter to identify every piece in that set. Marking the larger pieces would suffice. Also, majolica wares produced in the late nineteenth and early twentieth centuries as promotional items, souvenirs, and fair prizes were left largely unmarked. There was little value for a potter in identifying himself or his firm with such wares.

When majolica items bear no manufacturers' marks, cannot be positively identified as the works of a single firm (many firms produced surprisingly similar items), and will not even fit comfortably under the broad headings "English, Continental, or American," they *will* end up here in this admittedly vague category (yet eminently *safe* category from an author's point of view): "Unattributed."

If anyone should have a positive identification for any of the unattributed pieces displayed in this book (i.e. the same piece displaying the manufacturer's mark of a particular firm, etc.), please write to me in care of the publisher and I will see that the item is properly attributed in later additions. I thank you all now for those generous future contributions!

Small mottled shell and coral basket. 4" h. $150+

Cachepots

Cachepot is a French term for an decorative pot that hides a much more utilitarian flower pot within it. For those who are wondering, the French term jardiniere, on the other hand, refers to a large, ornamental pot used either for growing flowers or holding cut flowers grown elsewhere.

English

An elaborate bamboo patterned cachepot, further adorned with a cobalt ribbon and bow, and accompanied by an underplate not shown in this image. This cachepot was produced by Minton and measures 9" high x 9" in diameter. $1100+

Candleholders

English

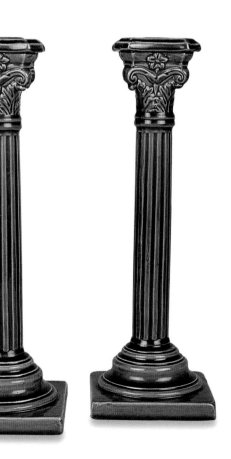

This pair of dark green candlesticks produced by James Wardle & Company measure 11.5" high each. The Staffordshire pottery firm James Wardle & Company of Hanley produced a variety of wares (including majolica) from 1854 to 1935 under a variety of company names. Company names and dates included: J.W. Wardle, 1854-1871; Wardle & Co., 1871-1903; Wardle & Co. Ltd., 1903-1909; Wardle Art Pottery Co. Ltd., 1910-1935. $400-650

Continental

A pair of Sarreguemines dark green candlesticks. 6.5" h. $400-650

Floral candleholder, 6" h. $300-330

Figural monkey candle-
stick, 5"h. $400-650

Pig with a purple smoking jacket figural candlestick, 7.5" h. $400-650

Cat with mice figural candlestick,
7.5" h. $500-700

Clocks

Unattributed

A cobalt glazed, floral decorated mantle
clock. 9" h. $400-440

A largely cobalt glazed mantle clock adorned
with a scene featuring a pleasant encounter
between a gentleman and a lady. 13" h.
$400-440

Ewers

English

Minton Satyr turquoise ewer with a strap and garland handle. 18″ h. $4500+

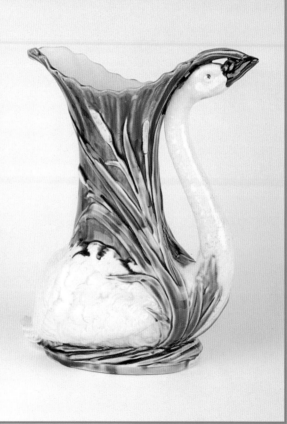

A swan and cattail ewer, English. 12″ h. This ewer sold at auction for $2000.

Continental

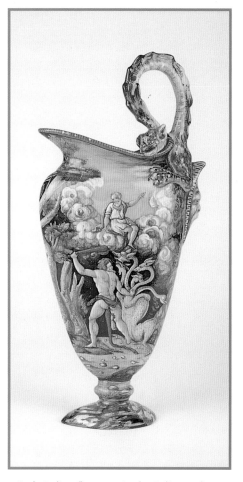

Portuguese Palissy style ewer decorated with applied water lilies, leaves, and medallions featuring either lobsters or crabs. 13.5″ h. $750+

Early Italian flat ewer in the Palissy style featuring a scene of a man fighting a five-headed dragon. This ewer also features a dragon handle. The base displays an unidentified blue rooster mark. 13.5″ h. $1200+

Continental cobalt ewer with a painted panel featuring women at leisure. 12″ h. $150+

Inkwells

Unattributed

This water lily inkwell is missing its lid. $115+

Jardinieres

English

Minton Louis XVI style jardiniere adorned with wreath and bow knot ribbon handles. 15.5" h. x 18.5" w. $5250+

A large, oval, footed jardiniere with a cobalt background and birds, branches, and cattails decorative motifs. This piece has been attributed to Thomas Forester (Church Street Works, Longton, Staffordshire, 1877-1883; Thomas Forester & Son(s) (Ltd.), Phoenix Works, Longton, Staffordshire, c. 1884-1959). 17.5" l. $1500+

Unattributed

An impressive oval jardiniere supported by three winged figures, decorated with three cobalt medallions featuring birds, and a turquoise ground with pink ribbons and bows. Very much in the Anglo-French style of early English majolica but completely unidentified! 13.5" h. x 13.5"d. This piece sold at auction for $3000.

Jardiniere with open lattice work. 10" h. x 11.5" d. $525+

A rather primitive jardiniere with a woman profiled in a medallion. 6.5" h. x 6.5" d. $525+

Planters

English

A cobalt glazed, squirrel and bird decorated, square planter supported by four bird legs with ball and claw feet, produced by Joseph Holdcroft (another one of Herbert Minton's apprentices who went on to do well on his own). 3.75" h. x 4" d. $900+

Continental

A French Palissy ware rustic planter decorated with a bird's nest, eggs, and an egg stealing snake, all on a lush bed of leaves and ferns. 4.5" h. x 7" w. x 6" d. $2400+

A French Palissy style square planter decorated with cobalt panels of oak leaves, ferns, and cattails, through which a butterfly flits. 4" h. $300+

A Continental planter featuring floral and leaf decorations. $175-200

Plaques

Scottish

Palissy ware oval plaque by Thomas Shirley & Co. (Greenock, Scotland, c. 1840-1857; thereafter Clyde Pottery Co., c. 1857-1862). 9" l. $3600+

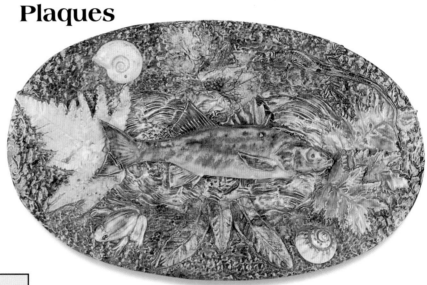

Continental

Continental plaque featuring a pleasant family boating scene. 9" x 11.25". $425-470

Unattributed

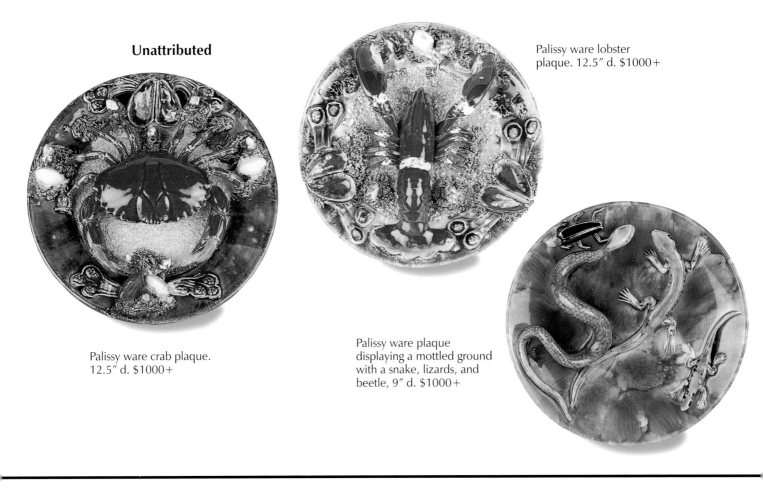

Palissy ware lobster plaque. 12.5" d. $1000+

Palissy ware crab plaque. 12.5" d. $1000+

Palissy ware plaque displaying a mottled ground with a snake, lizards, and beetle, 9" d. $1000+

Tiles

For a good look at English majolica tile in situ in fine old English and Irish public spaces, see Dawes 1990, pp. 12-20.

Continental

Continental chicken with chicks tile. 5". $100-150

American

Majolica tile advertising "The M. S. Huey Co. Wood Mantels, 551 Mass Av., Indianapolis." 6" d. $200-300.

Unattributed

Round floral tiles. 3.5" d. $100-150 each

Trays

English

A beautiful Wedgwood cobalt tray decorated with an attached blue bird, flowers and leaves on the rim. 10" w. This tray sold at auction for $2100.

Unattributed

Three figural trays (ashtrays?) featuring clothed creatures, two frogs and possibly a turkey. $165-180 each

Smoking Accessories

Cuspidors/spittoons

The Victorian hostess faced a serious problem. Tobacco chewers were notorious for spitting wherever and whenever convenient, with no apparent attempt to aim for any particular recepticle. No doubt hostesses fervently hoped chewers' eyes would be attracted to brightly colored majolica spittoons and that they would actually use them!

American

Shell-and-seaweed cuspidor by Griffen, Smith & Company. 6.5″ h. $800+

English

Humidors/Tobacco Jars

A humidor is a case designed to store cigars and keep the air within properly humidified. A tobacco jar is a covered jar designed to hold tobacco and is, at times, in the shape of a head, the top of which forms a cover. These items have been called both, and would serve the purpose in either case. Whatever *you* choose to call them, they are fascinating objects to collect.

This figural tobacco jar was made by Shorter and Sons (Stoke, Staffordshire, 1905 onward; previously Shorter & Boulton—under the S & B name, the firm began producing majolica wares in 1879). 4.75″ h. $250-275

American

Shell-and-seaweed tobacco jar by Griffen, Smith & Company. $950+

Continental/Unattributed

The vast majority of the unmarked, hence unattributed, tobacco jars were manufactured in Continental Europe. While it is difficult to identify these unmarked items with a particular firm, most have been attributed to European manufacturers in the past. The same situation exists with match boxes, match holders, and smoke sets.

An unusual figural elephant tobacco jar produced by Julius Strnact (Turn-Teplitz, 1882-c. 1914—known for the production of a variety of figural tobacco jars and using a JS initial maker's mark). 6″ h. $715-785; however, this piece sold at auction for $1400.

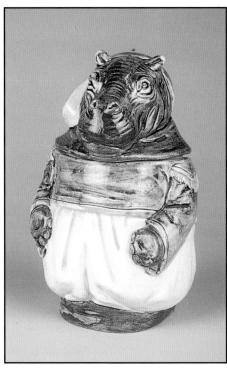

Julius Strnact hippo tobacco jar. 7.25" h. $715-785; however, this piece sold at auction for $1500.

JS initial manufacturer's mark of Julius Strnact, 1882-c. 1914.

This tobacco jar features a "marvelously" pompous man in a fur coat, gray suit, and a top hat. It was produced by Julius Strnact. 8" h. $500-600

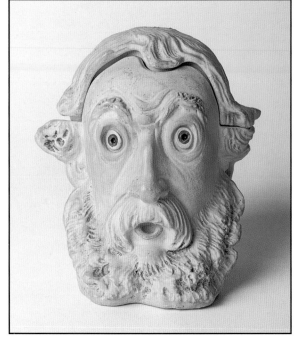

An odd bisque bearded man tobacco jar by Wilhelm Schiller and Son. $300+

Continental tobacco jar featuring a scene of man smoking a pipe. This tobacco jar has a molded pipe on the lid for a handle. $175-195

Continental tobacco jars fashioned as jugs with pipes leaning against them. $175-195 each.

A very well executed figural tobacco jar: a full bust of a man with a goatee and outstretched hands. 11″ h. x 10.5″ w. This unusual piece sold at auction for $1250.

Woman with bonnet tobacco jar, signed "Hoganas." 9" h. $350-450

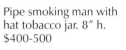

Pipe smoking man with hat tobacco jar. 8" h. $400-500

Humorous man in a brown jacket and top hat tobacco jar. $300

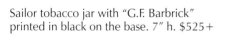

Sailor tobacco jar with "G.F. Barbrick" printed in black on the base. 7" h. $525+

Elf seated atop a log tobacco jar. $225+

Brownie with purple jacket tobacco jar. 6.5"
h. $350-385

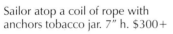

Sailor atop a coil of rope with
anchors tobacco jar. 7" h. $300+

The Indians and Middle Eastern
figures may be grouped under designs
termed "Des Indes." Indian chief
seated atop a square tobacco jar with
a scene of an Indian chief on the side.
8.25"h. $295-325

An unusual camel and Middle
Eastern smoker figural
tobacco jar. 7" h. $300+

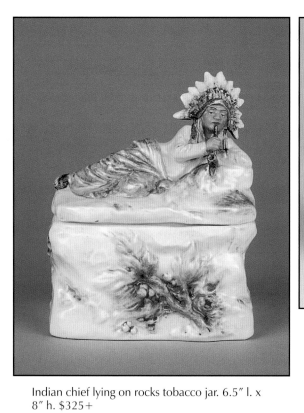

Indian chief lying on rocks tobacco jar. 6.5″ l. x 8″ h. $325+

Brown Indian head tobacco jar. 5″ h. $110+

Large Indian tobacco jar. 9″ h. $290-320

Indian chief tobacco jar. $290-320

Indian tobacco jar. 8″ h. $290-320

Middle Eastern figure tobacco jar. 9" h. $290-320

Small Middle Eastern figure tobacco jar. $290-320

Man with cap tobacco jar. 4.5" h. $565-620

Jockey tobacco jar. 5.5" h. $565-620

A cigar smoking man in a multi-colored hat tobacco jar. 5.5" h. $250-275

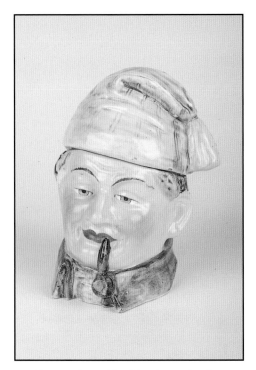

Pipe smoker with a blue hat and yellow tassel tobacco jar. $250-275

I wouldn't trust either of the characters depicted on these tobacco jars! $250-275 each

Two convivial monks rendered as tobacco jars. 8.5" h & 5.5" h. respectively. $310-340 each

Bemused man in a green hat tobacco jar. $310-340

Jester and clown tobacco jars. $310-340 each

Hooded man tobacco jar. $250-275

These three gents would be considered "local color" around town. **Left:** $260-290; **Right:** $400-440; **Below:** $260-290.

The Express goes nowhere today! Napping Express train engineer tobacco jar. 7" h. $450+

You'll get there faster with this determined motorist! $400-440

Mustachioed pipe smoker tobacco jar. $280-310

Two smoking gents in caps. 9" h. $565-620; $280-310

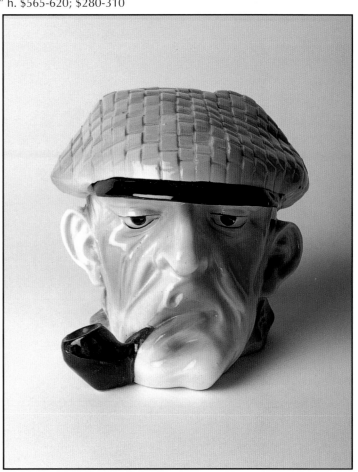

For when the game is afoot! Sherlock Holmes tobacco jar. 10.5″ h. $825+

Variations on a theme. 7.5″ h. each. $325-360 each

Women from the Far East. $300+ each

Young woman with golden tresses and a red scarf around her head. $190+

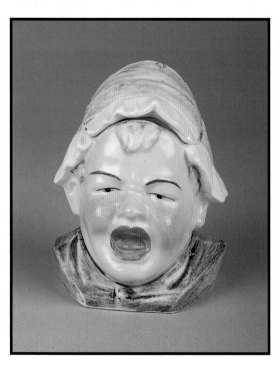

Two moods of toddlers. $175-195 each.

Large buffalo in green smoking jacket with pipe tobacco jar, 8.5" h. $800+

Welcome to the menagerie! Don a smoking jacket and come along. Bear with blue smoking jacket and pipe tobacco jar. $450+

Wild cat tobacco jar. 7.5″ h. $800+

Large cat with a bird in its mouth tobacco jar. 8.5″ h. $550+

Left: Cat playing with ball of yarn tobacco jar. 4.5″ h. $575+

Right: Cat and dog in basket tobacco jar. 5.75″ h. $790+

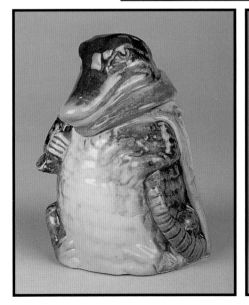

Left: Crocodile with red cape and pipe tobacco jar. 5″ h. $475+

Right: Large crocodile tobacco jar. 6.5″ h. $550+

Bulldog tobacco jar. 7.5" h. $265+

Dog tobacco jar. 6.5" h. $450+

Dog with red smoking jacket tobacco jar. 6" h. $675+

Bulldog with red smoking jacket tobacco jar, mint, 8". $750+

Spaniel tobacco jar. $600+

Bulldog with red cape and
turban tobacco jar. 6″ h.
$750+

Variations on a theme. Bulldogs with blue smoking jackets and mugs tobacco jars. 6" and 7.5" h. $675-775

Bulldog head tobacco jars. 5.5" & 4.5" h. $450+ each

Left: Hunting dog head tobacco jar. 5" h. $415+

Right: Dog atop a mottled box tobacco jar with cobalt accents. 5.5" h. x 5.5" l. $640+

Elephants in red smoking jackets tobacco jars. 8" h., 7" h., and 6" h. $550-750

Triple elephant tobacco jar.
8.5″ h. $375+

Fox tobacco jar. 5″ h. $600+

Fish with cigars in purple smoking jackets tobacco jars. 7″ h. and 8.5″ h. $600-800 depending on size.

Mandolin playing frog tobacco jar. 6″ h. $600+

Crouching, croaking frogs
in red smoking jackets
tobacco jars. 4"h., 5.5" h.
$470-520

Frog with red smoking jacket and
pipe tobacco jar. $500-800

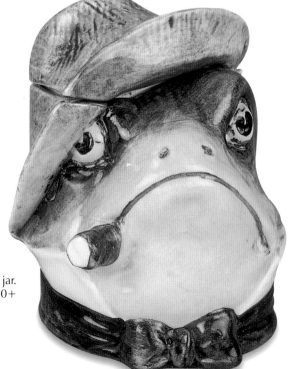

Frog's head tobacco jar.
4.25" h. $450+

Large hippo tobacco jar. 5″ h. x 7.5″ l. $650+

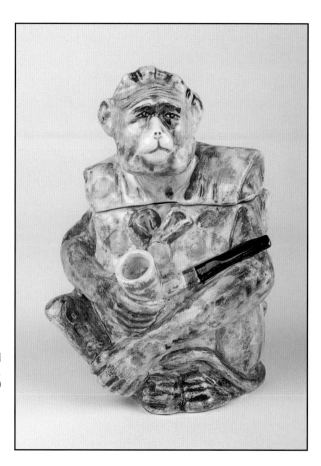

Monkey with pipe and red
smoking jacket tobacco jar. 7.5″ h.
$775-850

Monkey head tobacco jar. 5.25" h. $450+

Monkey head tobacco jar. 4.25" h. $250+

"Madam owl's" head tobacco jar, with a pink bonnet and turquoise bow, possibly by Strnact. 4.5" h. $450+

Three piglets atop a pig tobacco jar. $450+

Owl tobacco jar. 7" h. $450+

Pigs with pipes in tobacco jars. 6" h. each. $550-675

Pig with red coat and walking stick tobacco jar. 6.5" h. $750+

Pig shop keeper tobacco jar, with blue apron and broom. 7.5" h. $675+

Well dressed pig couple tobacco jar. 6" h. $750+

Left: Pig's head tobacco jar. 5.5" h. $450-495

Right: Tiger head tobacco jar. The hat reads "Dick." 5.5" h. $345-380

Three Art Nouveau tobacco jars. $175-225 each.

Round tobacco jar with scenes of people in relief. There are hallmarks on the silver lid. $185-205

Octagonal scenic
tobacco jar. $185-205

Continental tobacco jar
with a molded scene in
which a frog playing a
mandolin rides a fish.
The jar is topped with a
water lily lid. 7″ h.
$300-330

Square tobacco jar with skull in a riding cap lid finial
and a scene of pipe smoking cyclists on base. $185-205

A variety of tobacco jars decorated in the Art Nouveau style. 4″-6.25″ h. $175-225 each.

Art Nouveau style tobacco jar with a pipe and a cap on the lid. $175-225

A closer look at an Art Nouveau style round tobacco jar with pipe on the lid. 6″ h. $175-225

Still concerned about whether to call these humidors or tobacco jars? With a bundle of cigars for the body and a pipe on the lid, it is apparent the manufacturer was not! 6.25″ h. $175-225

Match Boxes / Match Holders

Unattributed

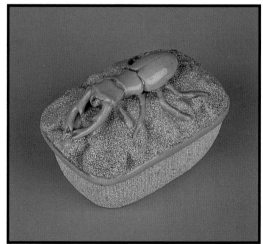

Unusual sand majolica/yellow ware insect covered match box with a striker under the lid. 3.5″ h. $265+

Blackamor match holder with striker. $300+

Boy at tree trunk match holder and striker. $150+

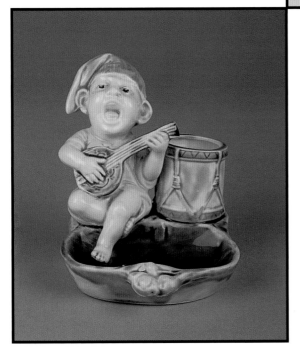

Impish mandolin playing soloist with drum match holder and striker. $115+

Deer match holder with striker. $190+

Castle match holder with striker. A similar example was produced by Moehling. 5″ h. $200+

Smoke Sets

Continental

Gnome with hammer smoke set by B. Bloch and Company, Eichwald, Bohemia. The company used either a "BB" or a "BB Austria" mark. $200-250

Unattributed

Left: Monk with mug smoke set. $500-550

Right: Indian scout smoke set, lacking a feathered headdress. 9.5″ h. $375-415 complete.

Boy rolling snowballs smoke set. $400-440

Brownie policeman smoke set. 8" h. $525+

Blackamor smoke set with impressed "Colorado Fina." $470-520

Blackamor smoke set with impressed "Cuba Fina" in several places. $565+

Pipe smoking figure on pillow smoke set. $470-520

Young man and young lady seated on benches with barrels behind them, smoke sets. 8.5" h. $300+ each

Bemused individuals with pipes and large bow ties, smoke sets. $450+ each

Bottom left: Bulldog with red hat and baskets smoke set. $300+

Bottom right: A pair of foxes under a tree with a bird smoke set. $825+

Frog with mandolin smoke set.
$340+

Unusual monkey atop a
log smoke set. 7" h.
$750+

Spill Vases

Spill vases were used to hold paper tapers or kindling wood termed "spills." Spills were used to transfer a small blaze from the fire to another source. During the nineteenth century, spill vases were often figural.

English

Minton figural spill vase portraying a lady vintager. This piece is shape number 283. (See the Introduction for two additional fine examples of Minton's figural spill vases.) $1500+

Umbrella Stands

English

The cobalt background draws attention to the bamboo and floral decorations adorning this well crafted umbrella stand by Joseph Holdcroft. 22″ h. $4000+

Vases, Urns and Ornamental Figures

English

Triple lion vase attributed to Thomas Forester. 8″ h. $900+

A pair of magpies by Mintons. 21.5″ h. These magpies sold for $2000 at auction.

Mintons England manufacturer's mark. An s was added to the Minton name on marks in 1873. England would be added to the mark in 1891. The Mintons name in manufacturers' marks would be in use from 1873-1951.

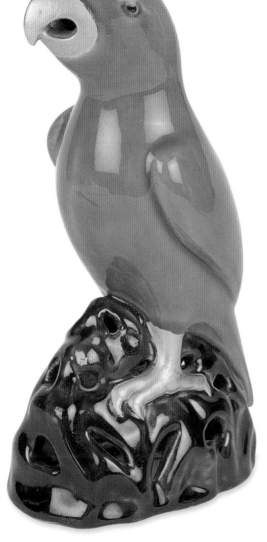

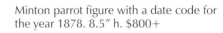
Minton parrot figure with a date code for the year 1878. 8.5" h. $800+

Continental

Gerbing and Stephan oval manufacturer's mark. Although difficult to make out in this example, the oval contains a suspension bridge with twin tower supports running through the center and the letter G above the center of the bridge, between the two supports. Gerbing and Stephan was founded in Bodenboch, Bohemia, after Schiller and Gerbing disbanded in 1885. The firm produced majolica wares from 1885 to c. 1910.

Gerbing and Stephan vase. 15" h. $300-330

Large Sarreguemines double handled urn, multi-colored in green, red, brown, and yellow. 17" h. $490+

Large Continental vase in the Art Nouveau style. 21" h. $750+

Two Continental vases. $100-150 each

Three Continental vases in the Art Nouveau style. $150-165 each

A pair of Continental figural vases. 6" h. each. $135-165 each

A pair of Italian majolica Blackamor figural vases with cornucopias. 20" h. $300+ each

Two Continental golfer vases. 6" h. each. $135-165 each

Continental vase featuring a woman beneath a tree. 12″ h.
$300-330

A pair of monumental Continental figures of a gentleman and lady in period dress. Each 30″ h.
NP (**N**o **P**rice)

Continental parrot on rock figural
vase. 7.5" h. $300+

Continental stork vase.
11.5" h. $225+

Continental peacock vase. 17.5"
h. x 13" w. NP (**N**o **P**rice)

Continental cat figural vase. 5.5" h.
$300+

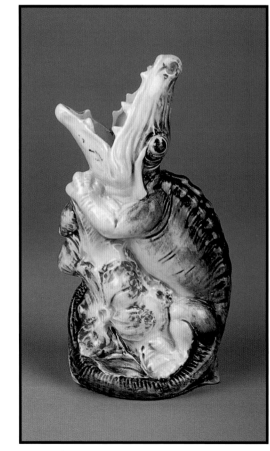

Continental crocodile vases. Each
6" h. $265+ each

Continental Art Nouveau three-part floral vase. 15″ w. $825+

A Palissy-style boat with an intertwined multi-colored snake, marked "G & St." Wares bearing the "G & St." mark have been considered to be of Central European origins. While no specific pottery has been identified, wares so marked are well made. 6″ x 9″. $900+

Unattributed

Sand vase. 2.75″ h.
$60-70

Blackamor figural vase.
18.5″ h. $700+

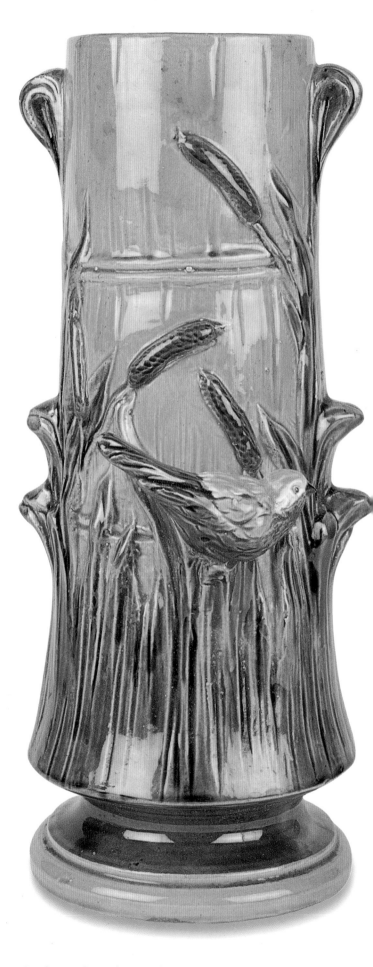

Bamboo and cattail vase with an applied bird. 13.5″ h. $425-470

Wall Bracket Shelves

A pair of Minton "Satyr" wall bracket shelves: one carrying a fox and the other with a variety of game animals. Both feature green and yellow oak leaves and acorn hanging over the satyrs' heads and each satyr is wrapped in gray fur. The Minton date code indicates a date of 1867 for these shelves. Each 18.5" h. This set sold for $16,000 at auction. Expect to pay $12,000 or more for each of these shelves on the secondary market

Wall Pockets

Continental

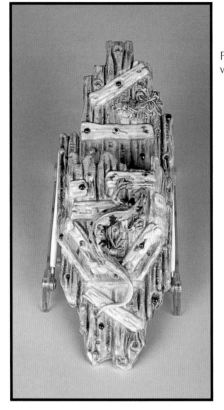

French Palissy ware picket fence wall pocket with lizard. 9.5" h. $1050+

American

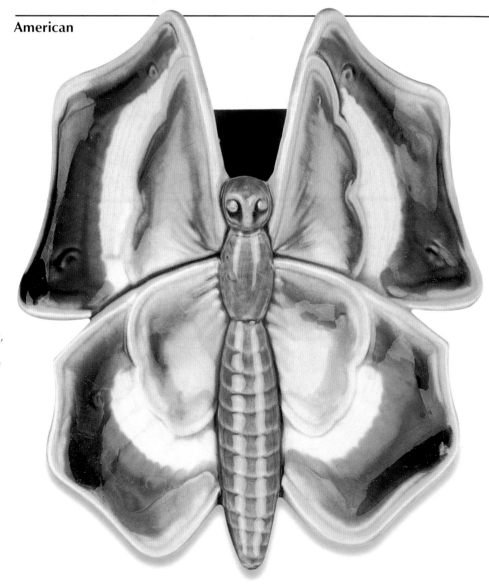

An extraordinary butterfly wall pocket with cobalt, yellow, white, and brown wings by Griffen, Smith & Company. This very rare item sold for $3500 at auction.

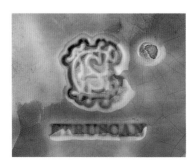

One of four different marks used by Griffen, Smith & Company during their years of majolica production. The firm was established in 1879, began majolica production in 1882, and the partnership changed in 1889, creating a new firm: Griffen, Love & Company.

PLACE STAMP

─── For the Table and for Tea ───

Asparagus Holders

Continental

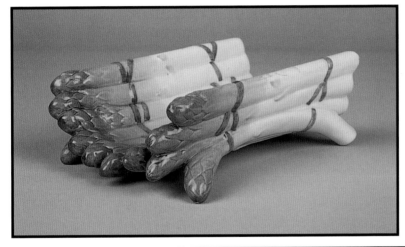

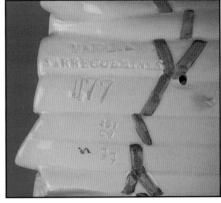

Sarreguemines asparagus cradle and mark.
Cradle 8.5″ long. $680-760

Bottles / Decanters

Continental

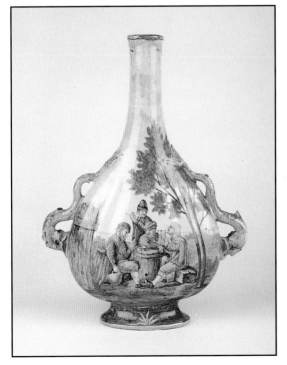

Early Italian bottle with serpent
handles and a painted scene.
13″ h. $150+

Continental pinecone
bottle. 9″ h. $100+

St. Clément duck decanter. The St. Clément pottery was established in the town of the same name in France in 1758. By 1892, the factory was purchased by Keller and Guérin (owners of Lunéville—known for its production of majolica asparagus plates and coffee services). St. Clément was known for the production of fine majolica figures with soft, blended glaze colors. St. Clément was purchased in 1922 by the Fenal family. Most wares were marked either KG (for the owners) or SC (for the company) on the base. 12.5" h. $300-330

St. Clément parrot decanter. 12" h. $300-330

Figural bottle featuring a dog with a rifle slung over the shoulder. 12.5" h. $1000+

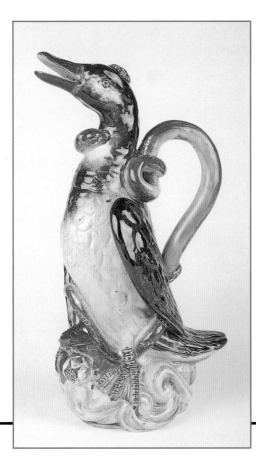

Figural duck decanter with serpent handle. 14″ h. $300-330

Bowls

English

Holdcroft water lily punch bowl.15″ d. x 7″ h. $2250+

Continental goose & gosling covered jar.
5.5" h. x 5" d. $675+

American

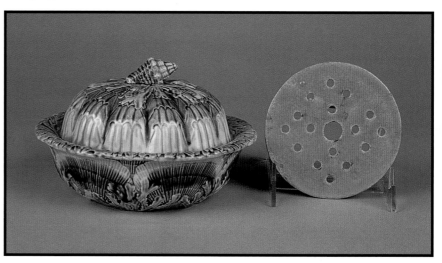

Shell-and-seaweed covered butter dish with insert by
Griffen, Smith & Company. $1125+

Unattributed

Rabbits in cabbage covered butter dish,
unglazed. 5" high. (To see an additional
example of this covered butter dish, with a
different glaze treatment and the insert visible,
see Snyder et al. 1994, p. 55.) $900+

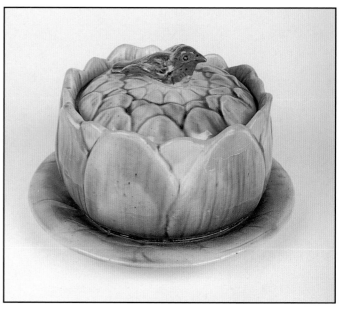

Bird atop an artichoke covered butter
dish. $475-525

Butter Pats

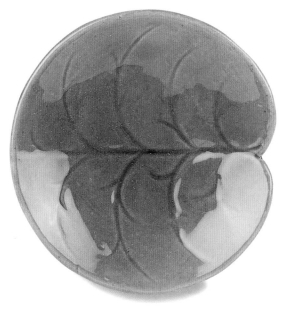

George Jones pond lily
butter pat. 3″ d. $325+

Simon Fielding ribbon and bow
decorated butter pat. 3″ d. This rare
piece brought $550 at auction.

Wedgwood sunflower
butter pat. 3″ d. $325+

American

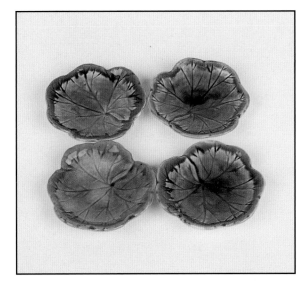

Geranium butter pats by Griffen, Smith &
Company. Each 3″ d. $135-165 each

Unattributed

Fish butter pat. 4.5" x 3.25". $500+

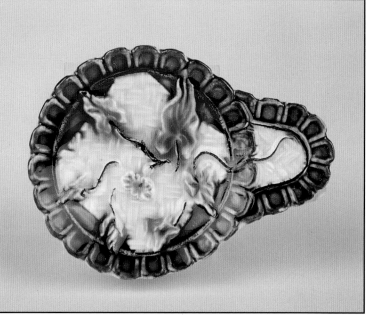

Morning glory on napkin butter pat with handle. 3.75". $135-150

Cobalt and yellow pansy butter pats. 3" d. $95-105

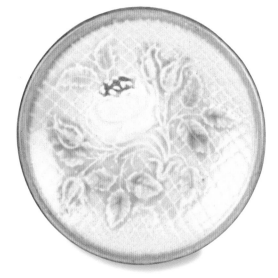

Rose on basket butter pat. 3" d. This butter pat sold at auction for $500.

Leaf shaped butter pat. $125-145

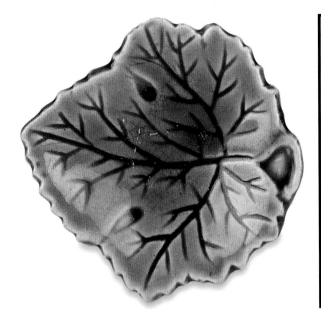

Green leaf butter pat. 3" d. $125-145

Butter pat in wire and metal frame basket with handle. $250-300

Cake Stands / Comports

English

Holdcroft comport featuring a boy on a rock base supporting the bowl in his upraised hands. 8" h. x 6.75" d. $1950+

Wedgwood footed comport. $750+

Continental

Large Continental floral comport. 14" d. x 8" h. $275-300

Large B. Block and Company shell comport, simply marked "Eichwald." $275-300

Continental comport adorned with leaves, flowers, and a molded basketweave center. 4.5" x 9". $300+

Cauliflower cake stand by Griffen, Smith & Company. 4" h. x 9" d. $600+

Maple leaves on a pink ground cake stand by Griffen, Smith & Company. 5.5" h. x 9.5" d. $250+

Grape leaf comport by Griffen, Smith & Company. 4" h. x 9.25" d. $395-435

Variation on the theme: maple leaves on a white ground cake stand by Griffen, Smith & Company. 5" h. x 9.5"d. $325+

Most impressive Minton centerpiece. This centerpiece sold at auction for $8250.

Cheese Keepers

English

Brownhills Pottery Company (Tunstall, Staffordshire, c. 1872-1896) cheese keeper, shown here with a dinner set. The decorative motif chosen reflects the Japanese influence. NP (**N**o **P**rice)

George Jones picket fence and apple blossom cheese keeper, 8.5"h, great color, mint. $3600+

Continental

Choisy mug featuring rabbits and a rabbit handle. $450+

American

Oak mugs by Griffen, Smith & Company. $375-425 each

Unattributed

Shell-and-seaweed shaving mug. $525+

Floral mug with a molded bamboo motif handle. $115+

Picket fence and leaf mug. $150+

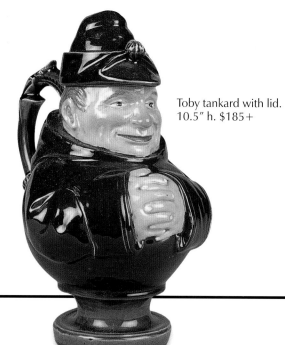

Toby tankard with lid. 10.5" h. $185+

Pitchers / Jugs

English

Pitcher by Joseph Holdcroft. 8.25" h. $375-415

Honey bear pitcher by Joseph Holdcroft. 10" h. (See Karmason et al. 1989, p. 104-107 for additional Holdcroft examples.) $675+

Minton tower pitcher with a pewter lid with a Jester finial, shape number 1231. 13" h. $1700+

Bamboo and fern pitcher by James Wardle & Co. (Shelton and Hanley, Staffordshire, 1854-1935. Company history: J.W. Wardle: 1854-1871; Wardle & Co.: 1871-1903; Wardle & Co., Ltd.: 1903-1909; Wardle Art Pottery Co. Ltd.: 1910-1924. Marks: J.W.: 1854-1871; WARDLE: 1871 onward with ENGLAND added to the mark c. 1891.) 6.5" h. $415+

Frog on lily pad pitcher, unmarked but including an English registry mark. 5.25" h. $1500-1650

Bamboo and fern cream pitcher by James Wardle & Co. 4" h. $225+

Wedgwood Argenta bird and fan pitcher. 6.5" h. $415+

Continental

Sarreguemines "Judy" toby jug (number 3430). It was accompanied by Punch (number 3431). (To see Punch, see Cunningham 1997, p. 73.) 12" h. This example of Judy brought $900 at auction.

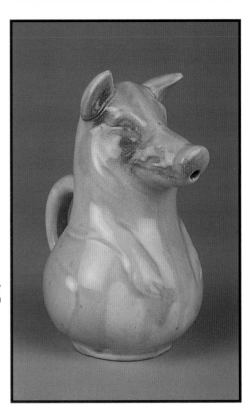

Pig pitcher (number 3318) by Sarreguemines. 8" h. $425-470

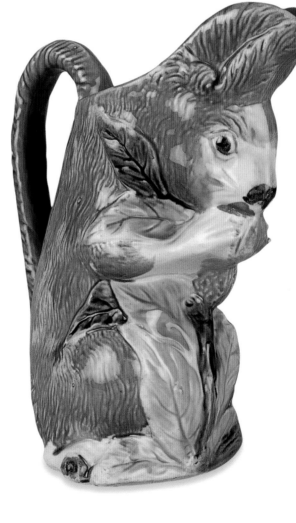

Squirrel with nut pitcher by Orchies (Orchies, France, c. 1886-1988. Mark: Circular mark with central windmill and printed ORCHIES MOULIN DES LOUPS HAMAGE around the circle's edge.). 9" h. $900-1000

Cat with mandolin pitcher by Orchies. 9.5" h. $700+

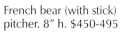
French bear (with stick) pitcher. 8" h. $450-495

Italian pitcher with mask spout, 12.5". $350+

Left: Continental pelican jug, drilled for lamp base. 6.5" h. $150+
Right: Continental frog jug with frog spout. 6.5" h. $375+

Portuguese hound handled game pitcher with a fox on the lid. 14" h. $675+

Face jug, Sarreguemines-type, possibly either French or German in origin. 8.5". $280-310

American

Sunflower pitcher by Griffen, Smith & Company. 8" h. This pitcher sold for $800 at auction.

Sunflower syrup pitcher with pewter lid and spout, Griffen, Smith & Co. $600-700 (add $300-330 more if the underplate is present)

Rustic jug by Griffen, Smith & Company. 8" h. $525+

Thorn jug by Griffen, Smith & Company. (See Karmason et al. 1989, p. 156 for additional examples.) $275-300

Acorn and oak leaf pitcher by Morley and Company. 5" h. $265+

Morley and Company fish pitcher with cobalt base. 8" h. $245-275

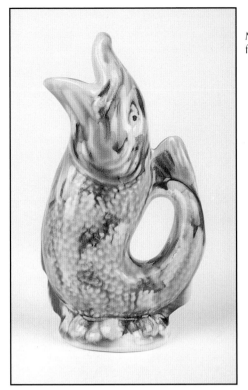

Morley and Company multi-colored fish pitcher. 6.5" h. $245-275

Unattributed

Pitcher with bird, leaves, and flowers motif on a basketweave background. 7" h. $400-440

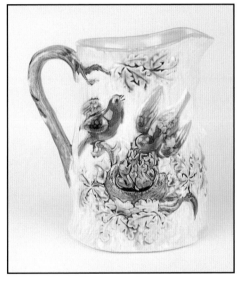

Birds feeding young in nest pitcher. 6" h. $400-440

Another example of the bird feeding young in nest motif adorns this pitcher. 7" h. $400-440

Mottled robin pitcher. 9.5" h. $495-585

Three stork in cattails pitchers, ranging in size from 9.25″, to 8.5″, and 7.25″ h. $950-1450+ by size

Fan and scroll pitcher. 6″ h. $265+

Pitcher decorated with leaves, flowers, and a bow. 7″ h. $395+

Basketweave pitcher with floral sprigs. 5.75" h. $215+

Pitcher with a floral sprig and fern motif. 8" h. $400+

Pineapple pitcher. 4" h. $275-300

Pineapple syrup pitcher with a pewter lid. 6.5" h. $750

Pineapple pitchers, 7.5″ and 8″ h.
$495-550

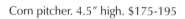

Corn pitcher. 4.5″ high. $175-195

Pitchers decorated in the same leaf motif with
different glaze treatments. 7″ h. $375+ each

Maple leaves on picket fence syrup
pitcher with a pewter lid. $415+

Unusual tree trunk jug with a lid and applied oak leaves and acorns. 14" h. NP

Seated bear pitcher, unattributed but featuring U.S. Patent No. 518205. 8.25" h. $415-455

Seated bear pitcher. 5.5" h. $375-415

Parrot pitcher, unattributed but possibly from one of the potteries in England's Staffordshire potting district. 9.5" h. $515-575

A different seated bear pitcher. 4.5" h. $375-415

Parrot pitcher, unattributed but possibly from England's Staffordshire potting district. 9.75". $515-575

Parrot pitcher, unattributed but possibly from England's Staffordshire potting district. 7.25" h. $515-575

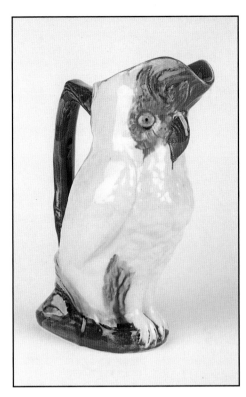

Parrot pitcher, a different style than one would expect from Staffordshire. 9" h. $515-575

Three variations on the owl decorative motif.
Left: Owl pitcher, unattributed but possibly potted by Nimy-les-Mons (Belgium 1797-1894 when the firm joins with Onnaing [just across the border in France] to create the Onnaing Society. Nimy marks include "Mouzin Freres," "Mouzin-Lecat" in a circular mark, and, at times, the second mark appears with the addition of "Cie" to the name). 11" h. $475-525
Center: Owl pitcher. 10.5" h. $400+
Right: Owl pitcher. 7" h. $400+

Owl pitcher. 7" h. $400+

Owl pitcher. 6.5" h. $400+

Pelican pitcher. Note the fish in the foremost pelican's mouth. 7.5" h. While this piece has been seen in the secondary market for $600-660, it sold for $1100 at auction.

Multi-colored owl pitcher, unattributed but similar to the work of Morley & Company of Wellsville and East Liverpool, Ohio. 6" h. While this owl pitcher sold at auction for $125, this author has seen similar unidentified owls command prices as high as $770.

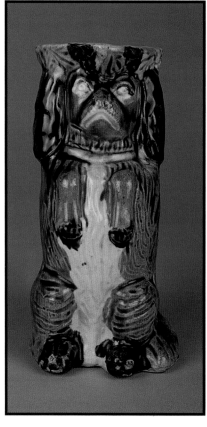

Spaniel pitcher. 7.25" h.
$450-500

Pug dog pitchers, unattributed but probably potted in England's Staffordshire district (however, there were similar pitchers made in the United States). 10.75" h., 8.5" h., 7.25" h. $400-600, depending on size.

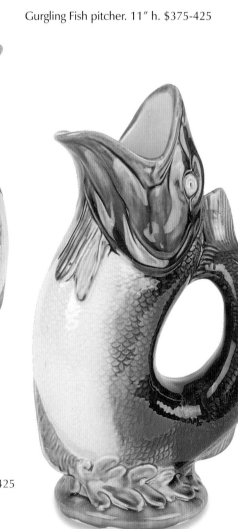

Gurgling Fish pitcher. 11" h. $375-425

Gurgling Fish pitcher. 13" h. Many potters made gurgling fish of varying qualities during the 1880s, including Thomas Forester in England, Onnaing in France, and Morley and Company in America. (See Cunningham 1997, pp. 43 & 105 for additional examples.) $375-425

Gurgling Fish pitcher. 11" h. $375-425

Gurgling Fish pitchers ranging in size from 9" to 9.75" h. $375-425

Monkey pitchers with bamboo handles in four sizes. 6.5" h.,
8" h., 9" h., 13" h. $650-$1200+ depending on size.

Four sided fish pitcher.
8.25" h. $375-425

Plates

You are about to encounter a wide variety of majolica plates with many forms of decoration; however, the oyster plates often capture more attention from collectors than most. Victorians were passionate about their oysters and ate them in staggering quantities! Desperate vendors often resorted to slipping a spoiled oyster in among a repeat serving to curb the appetite of an overindulgent oyster enthusiast. Oysters were held in such high esteem that they were served on plates specially designed to accomodate them. Different oyster plate styles were developed to allow the host and hostess to serve oysters in a variety of ways: on the half shell on ice, on the half shell without ice, or without the shells (to say nothing of oyster stew or oyster stuffing).

When serving oysters on the half shell on ice, a deep plate was required to hold the ice. Underplates were provided to catch the chilly water overflowing the plate as the ice melted. The oyster shell shaped wells into which the half shells rested when served on ice were smaller and deeper than on plates where ice was not required. When serving oysters on the half shell without ice, the plates were shallower, as were the wells. The wells themselves, as noted, were also larger. Unfortunately, oyster plates used to serve oysters on the half shell tended to be scratched by the rough outer surface of the shell itself.

The number of wells on oyster plates varied dramatically from one to six (one wonders if plates with fewer wells were purchased by penurious hosts and hostesses). Larger plates and platters could hold a more generous one to two dozen oysters. An ever impressive three tiered lazy susan designed by Minton held twenty-seven oysters!

English

George Jones shell oyster plate. 10" d. (If what you see here just is not enough, for additional examples of majolica oyster plates, see Karsnitz 1993, pp. 35-56.) This beautiful example sold at auction for $1600.

George Jones mottled oyster plate with raised center shell. 10.75″ d. This plate also sold for $1600 at auction.

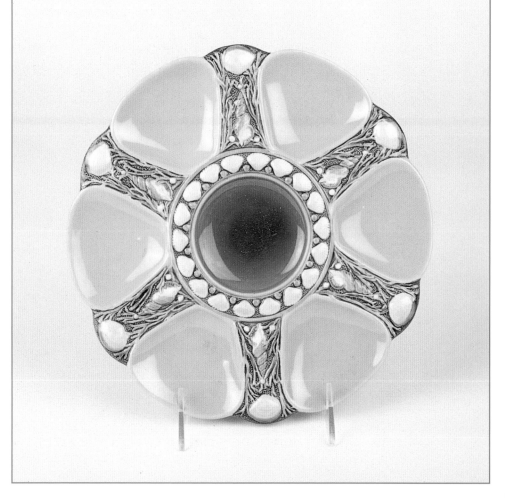

Oyster plate by Minton.
10″ d. $660-725

A rare Minton fish and shell seafood plate. Note the year cipher for 1872 to the right of the mark and the registration mark. 10″ d. This rare plate sold for $1400 at auction.

Wedgwood Argenta chrysanthemum plate. 9″ d. $415+

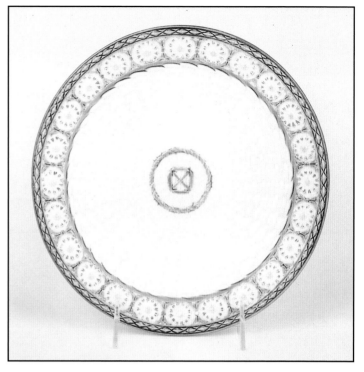

Wedgwood Argenta Stanley pattern plate. 9″ d. $325+

Wedgwood Argenta strawberry and leaf plate. 9″ d. $325+

Wedgwood turquoise butterfly and bee plate. 9″ d. $275+

Wedgwood cauliflower plate. 9" d. $400+

Wedgwood ocean plate with a gray border. 5" d. $300-330

Two Wedgwood dark green leaf plates. $200+ each

Continental

Choisy hen with chicks plate. 9" d. $375-415

Floral plate marked "Imperial Bonn" (Germany). 9.5" d. $95+

Oyster plate by Longchamp (Dijon, France. Used the marks: "LONGCHAMP" and "TERRE DE FER." Longchamp also produced fruit laden wall pockets and asparagus servers in majolica.). 9" d. (A set of six of these Longchamp oyster plates sold at auction for $1100.) $200-250

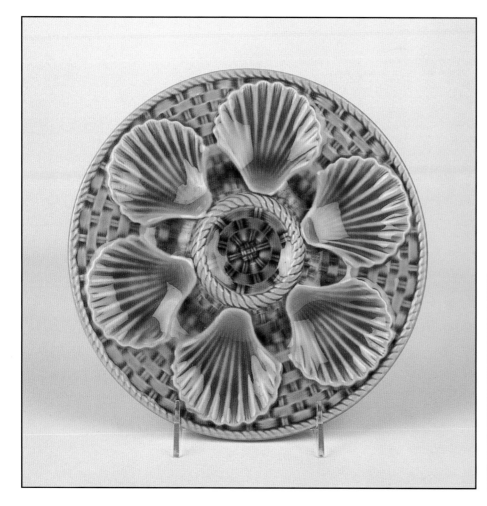

Longchamp oyster plate and printed shield and "LONGCHAMP FRANCE" manufacturer's mark. $200-250

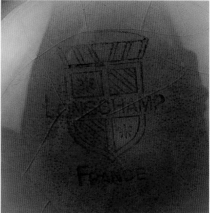

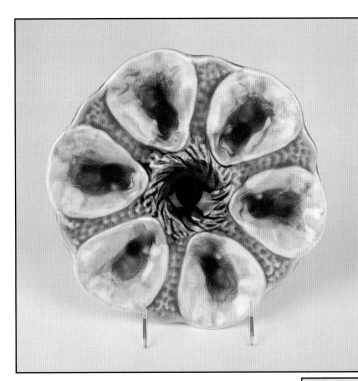

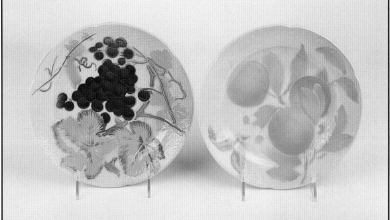

Orchies French majolica oyster plate marked with an impressed windmill and "ORCHIES" mark and an inked mark "MADE IN FRANCE." 9.5" d. $250-300

St. Clément fruit plates and mark. Each 8.5" d. $110-125 each (with hard to find fruit depicted on these plates going higher).

Sarreguemines green oyster plate. 10" d. $250-275

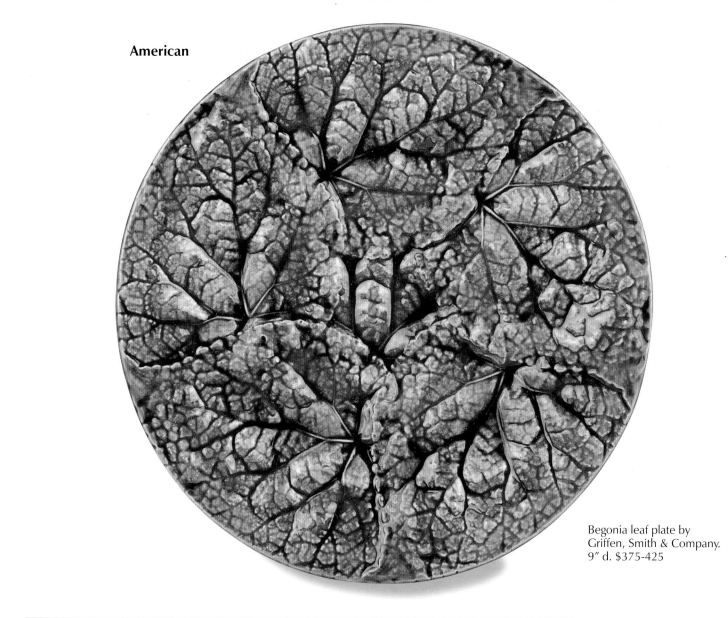

Begonia leaf plate by
Griffen, Smith & Company.
9" d. $375-425

Cauliflower plates, Griffen,
Smith & Company. 9.25"
d. $375-425 each

Three "Leaf on Plate" motif plates by Griffen, Smith & Company. 8", 8" and 9" d. $375-425

Grape motif plate, Griffen, Smith & Company. 6.25" d. $280-310

Cauliflower plate, Griffen, Smith & Company. 9" d. $375-425

Lily plate with cobalt center, Griffen, Smith & Company. 8" d. $290-320

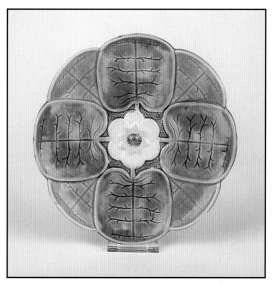

Lily plate, Griffen, Smith & Company. 9" d. $290-320

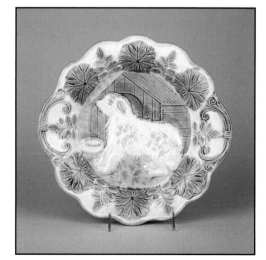

Dog and doghouse plate,
American. 10.75" d. $375-410

Unattributed

Green oyster plate. $225+

Oyster plate. 10″ d. $265+

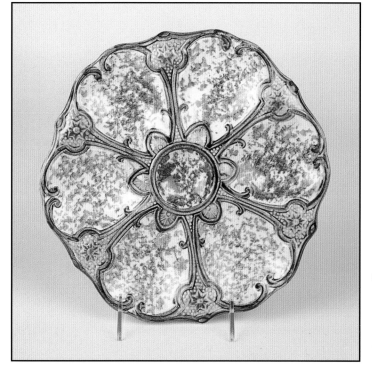

Oyster plate. 9.5″ d. $335+

Unusually shaped oyster plate with handle in pink, green, and yellow. 9" x 7.5". $450+

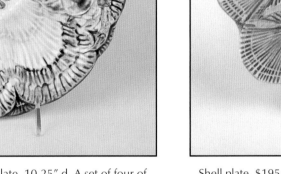

Eye-catching multi-colored oyster plate. 10.25″ d. A set of four of these plates sold for $2000 at auction.

Shell plate. $195+

Two portrait plates. Each 8″ d. $195+ each

Three plates featuring mythical characters in various activities. Red rims: 8″ d.; blue rim: 11.5″ d. $195+ (8" d.); $225+ (11.5" d.)

A scenic castle view decorates this 6.5" diameter plate, probably of Continental origins. $135+

Combined bird, fruit and foliage decorated plate. 10" d. $205+

Morning glory and napkin motif plate, probably Continental. 10" d. $205+

Cobalt, grape, and vine plate with an angel in the center. 9.25" d. $375+

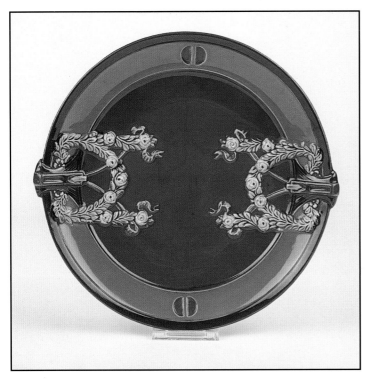

Garland draped 9" diameter plate. $280+

Leaf decorated 7.5" diameter plate. $150+

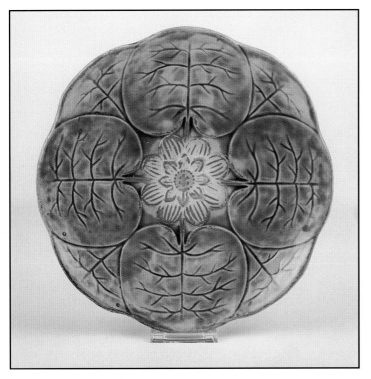

Water lily plate similar, but not identical in either molding or glazing, to the Griffen, Smith & Company water lily plates. 9" d. $125-140

Fruit and foliage motif plate. 9.5" d. 150+

Another colorful variation on the grape leaf and grape decorative motif adorns these 8.5" diameter plates. $150+ each

A similar flower and foliage plate in a metal frame basket. $275+

Platters

Continental

Green oyster platter by La Faïencerie de Gien (established 1864, producing majolica vases, plaques, plates and green dessert plates) with printed "GIEN FRANCE" mark. 12.5" d. $175-195

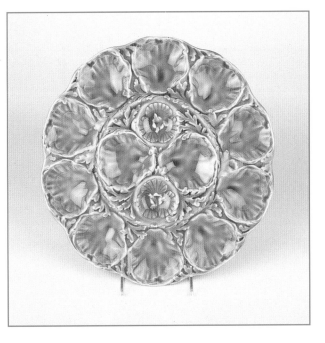

Longchamp green basket weave, white shell, and brown trim oyster platter, 13" diameter, and plate, 9.25" diameter. Platter: $175-195

St. Clément green and white oyster platter, 14″ diameter, and plate, 10″ diameter, with lemon centers. Platter: $175-195. $800 was paid at auction for a service with twelve plates and the platter.

St. Clément brown oyster platter, 14″ diameter, and plate, 10″ diameter, with impressed script manufacturer's mark. Platter: $175-195

Sarreguemines oyster platter, 14.5″ diameter, and plate, 9.5″ diameter. Platter: $175-195

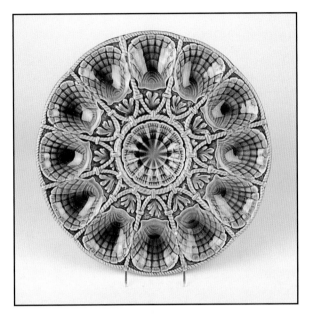

Sarreguemines oyster platter, 14.5" dia., and plate, 9.25" dia. Platter: $175-195

Sarreguemines oyster platters, 15" diameter (green) and 14.5" diameter (white). $175-195 each

Continental scenic charger (a.k.a. platter) with a cobalt ground. 14" d. $200+

Shell-and-seaweed platter, Griffen, Smith & Company. 14". $1375-1500

Unattributed

Unusually shaped shell oyster platter. 13.5". $900+

Cobalt fish platter with outstanding color. 13.5" l. This eye-catching platter sold for $1000 at auction.

Turquoise ground wild rose platter. 13″ l. $675+

Floral motif platter with an interesting form. 9″ x 11.5″. $485+

Cobalt grape platter. 11″ x 13″. $415+

Strawberry and bow platter with a turquoise ground. $500+

Leaf motif platter. 11.75" x 9". $470-520

Begonia leaf on basket platter with ribbon and bow handles. 14.5" l. $470-520

Begonia on cobalt platter with vivid color. 12" l. $750+

Begonia leaf platter. 11" l. $250-275

Salt Cellars

English

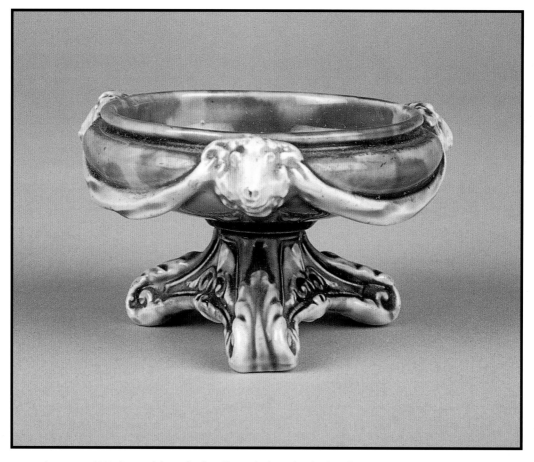

An unusual Wedgwood footed salt cellar with three lambs' heads and cobalt accents. $340+

Unattributed

Unusual squirrel atop leaves
salt cellar, 2.5" d. $225+

Sardine Boxes

American

Lily & Swan sardine box by Griffen, Smith & Company. Sardine boxes were certainly preferrable to the tins sardines came in when serving the delicacy at a dinner party. 3" x 5.5" x 3.75". $1320+

Unattributed

Pineapple sardine box.
$900-1000

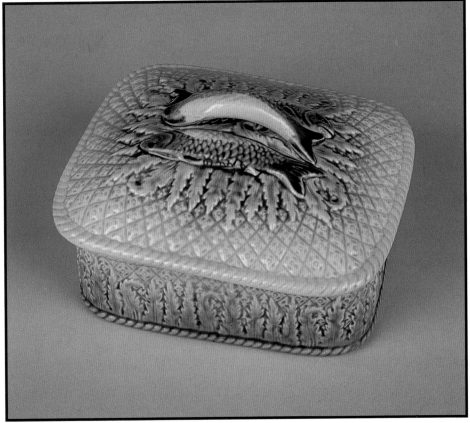

Sauce Dishes

American

Cosmos sauce dish by Griffen, Smith & Company. 5.5" d. $300+

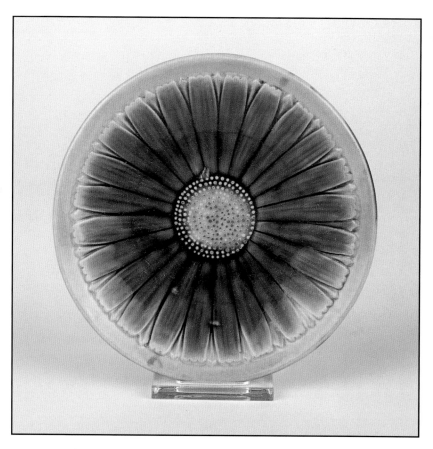

Shell-and-seaweed scalloped edge sauce dish by Griffen, Smith & Company. $375+

Servers

An impressive Minton four tier revolving oyster
server. 10.5" h. $4500-4950

Magnificent Minton twig strawberry server, complete with cream, sugar, and two strawberry spoons. 7.5" h. $4950-5280

This is a creamer from a strawberry server by Wedgwood. $100-110

Longchamp oyster server with center handle. 15″ l. x 5″ h. $1500+

American

Strawberry server by Griffen, Smith & Company. 8" x 10.5". (See Snyder et al. 1994, p. 130 for additional examples of this server by both Griffen, Smith & Co. and Wedgwood.) $775-975 as is. Complete with both the cream and sugar bowl, these items may reach $2250 in value.

Shakers

English

Wedgwood shaker with a cobalt rim. 3.5" h. $265+

Unattributed

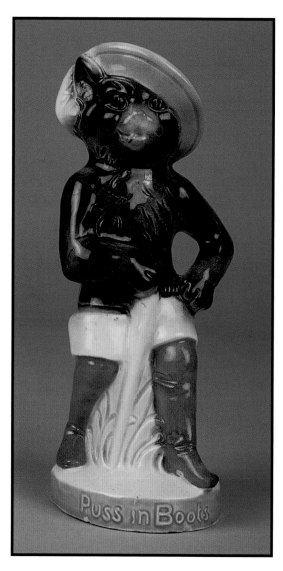

Puss n' Boots shaker. 7.5" h. $320+

Tea Sets

Isle of Man Union Jack three legged sailor teapot, attributed to William Brownfield & Sons (Cobridge, Staffordshire, 1850-1892) (For more about the company history and their marks, see Kowalsky 1999, p. 131), with molded inscription on base: "W. Broughton, 50 Duke St. Douglas," c. 1880. 8.5" h. $2090-2300

Isle of Man three legged sailor with rope handle teapot, attributed to William Brownfield & Sons, c. 1880. 9.5" h. (It pays to attend auctions. This piece and the Isle of Man Union Jack sold at auction in October 1999 for $750 each!) $2090-2300

Isle of Man three legged gentleman teapot, attributed to William Brownfield & Sons, c. 1880. 8.5" h. $2090-2300

Holdcroft mustache cup and saucer. $350-500

Minton cockerel teapot, shape no. 1909, date code for 1880. $3000-5000

Continental

Black poodle teapot stamp marked "Erphila Germany." 8.5". $260-285

American

Blackberry teapot by the Chesapeake Pottery Company (Baltimore, Maryland, c. 1882-1910), marked with the tradename Clifton and the DFH monogram of the company's founder, Donald Francis Haynes. $400+

Cobalt basket and floral tea set, attributed to the Eureka Pottery (Trenton, New Jersey, 1883-1887). 8" h. This set sold at auction for $800.

Corn creamer, Griffen, Smith & Company. 3.75"h. $185-200

Bamboo & fern teapot by Griffen, Smith & Company. $660-725

Cauliflower tea set, Griffen, Smith & Company. Teapot: 5.5" h.; saucer: 6" d. Teapot: $1230-1350. Cup and saucer: $250-275

Left: straight spout shell-and-seaweed coffee pot, Griffen, Smith & Company. 4.5" h. $1400-1800
Middle: shell-and-seaweed small teapot with crooked spout, Griffen, Smith & Company. 4.5" h. $1000-1400
Right: shell-and-seaweed large teapot with crooked spout, Griffen, Smith & Company. 7" h. $1000-1400

Shell-and-seaweed sugar, creamer, and spooner, Griffen, Smith & Company. Sugar: 5″ h. $825+

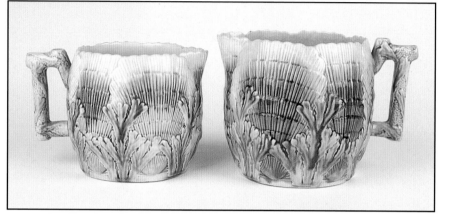

Shell-and seaweed pitchers, Griffen, Smith & Company. 6″ and 6.5″ h. $845-930 each.

Shell-and-seaweed mustache cup and saucer, Griffen, Smith & Company. Cup: 2.5″ h. $850-935

Shell-and-seaweed cup and saucer, Griffen, Smith & Company. Saucer: 6.25″ d.; cup: 2.5″ h. $375-415

Scarce bird's nest teapot with twig handle. $750+

Bird and iris teapot. $225+

Fish swallowing fish teapot. 11″ l. x 6″ h. $650-715

Cobalt fish teapot with fish lid
finial. 5″ h. $600+

Floral and basket motif three piece tea set. Teapot: $225+

Morning glory and napkin three piece tea set with cobalt accents, possibly Continental. Teapot: $225+

Cobalt blackberry three piece tea set. Teapot: $225+. This set sold for $500 at auction.

Wild rose and rope teapot. 7" h. $450+

Pink floral covered sugar bowl. $150+

Water lily covered sugar bowl. $200+

Drum shaped basketweave and floral motif teapot. 7" h. $450+

Pineapple three piece tea set. Teapot: $1055-1170

Pineapple three piece tea set. Teapot: 5.25" h. Teapot: $1055-1170

Pineapple tea kettle with bail handle. 8″ h. $1055-1170

Pineapple cup and saucer with beautiful glaze colors. $375+

Pineapple sugar bowl and creamer. $375+

Toothpick Holders

English

T. Sargent picket fence and leaf toothpick holder. 3″ h. $225-250

Unattributed

Ladies hat toothpick holder. 4.5" l. $225-250

Trays

English

George Jones palm and grape tray. 8.5". This tray sold at auction for $5000.

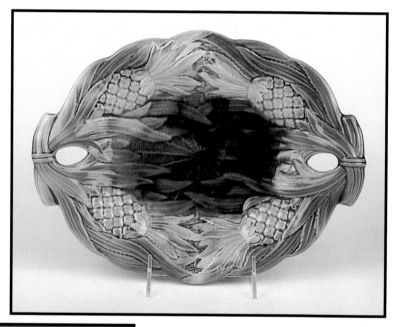

George Jones pineapple tray. 12". $1500+

Samuel Lear Classical Sunflower and Urn round handled tray with a lavender border. 11". $300+

Continental

Fruit tray by Reichard M. Krause (Schweidnitz, Silesia, c. 1882-? Mark: KM beneath crown. For additional Krause pieces, see Murray 1997, pp. 131-133.). 13" d. $225-250

American

Oak bread tray with pink border, Griffen, Smith & Company. $565-625

Morley & Company multi-colored leaf tray. 7.25" l. $150+

Morley & Company fish tray. 13" l. $475+

Wheat bread tray featuring the molded sentiment, "Eat thy Bread with Thankfulness." 12.5" l. $660-725

Begonia leaf bread tray, also reading, "Eat thy Bread with Thankfulness." 12.5" l. $660-725

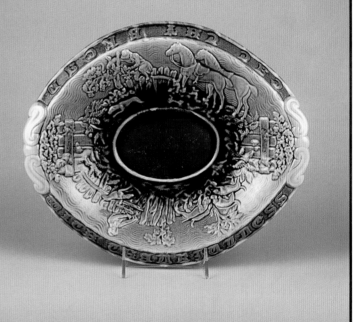

"Eat thy Bread with Thankfulness" bread tray featuring a farm scene in relief. 12.5" l. $660-725

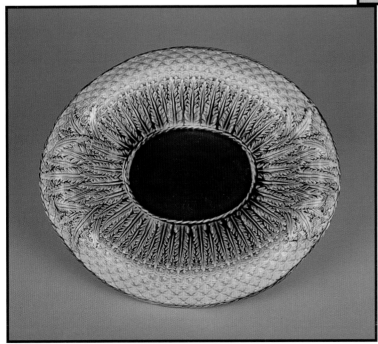

Pineapple bread tray. 13" l. $660-725

Wild rose and rope motif tray with a cobalt center. 8.25″ l. $400+

Cobalt wild rose round tray. 12″ d. $450+

Two fish trays. 7.5" x 9"; 6" x 7.75". $350+ each

Mottled begonia leaf tray, unattributed but very similar in design to a tray produced by Griffen, Smith & Company. 12" l. $350-385

Tureens

English

Minton lobster covered tureen, shape number 1523, with a date code for 1870. 14" l. This tureen sold at auction for $10,000!

Continental

Sarreguemines duck covered basket tureen. 11" l. $250-275

Sarreguemines fruit laden basket tureen. 9″ d. $465-510

Sarreguemines pansy covered basket tureen. 12″ l. $465-510

Basket tureen with cherries finial, attributed to Sarreguemines. 7.5" d. $250-275

French vegetable tureen with griffin handles and vegetables in relief. 12" h. x 13" w. $500-550

Portuguese duck tureen with duckling finial. $180-200

Continental tureen with an egg finial and a chicken with chicks, rabbit, and a bird in a nest of eggs in relief on the cover. 8" d. $250+

Continental chicken and rooster covered tureen. 6.5" d. x 7" h. $465-510

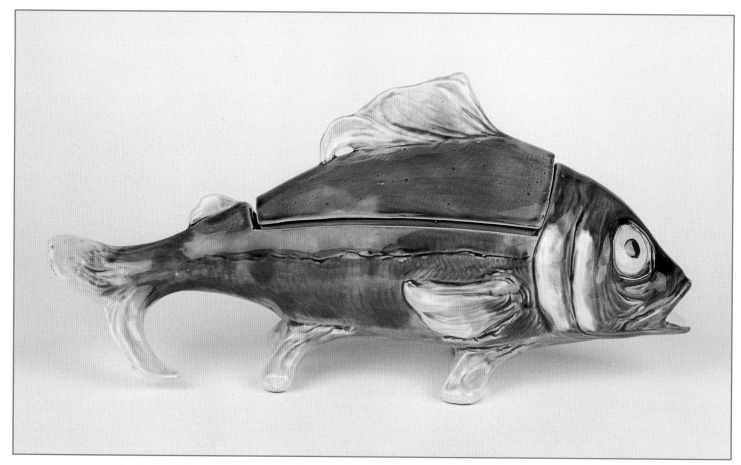

Continental fish covered tureen. 14" l. $250+

Continental tureen with fish, vegetables and leaves on the cover. 10" d. $180-200

A most unusual Continental tureen featurng rabbits in a basket. 9.5″ w. x 9″ h. $250+

Wine Coolers

Minton baluster form wine cooler with intertwined green cornucopia handles spilling colorful fruits and grapes, date code for 1868. 11" h. x 14" w. This wine cooler sold at auction for $1500.

Recommended Reading

The Arts Journal Illustrated Catalogue: The Industry of All Nations 1851. London: George Virtue, 1851.

Barber, Edwin Atlee. "Etruscan Majolica." *Bulletin of the Pennsylvania Museum*, Memorial Hall, Fairmount Park, Philadelphia, July 1907.

_____. *Marks of American Potters.* Philadelphia, Pennsylvania: Patterson & White Co., 1904.

Bergensen, Victoria. *Majolica: British, Continental, and American Wares 1851-1915.* London: Barrie & Jenkins, 1989.

Bockol, Leslie. *Victorian Majolica.* Atglen, Pennsylvania: Schiffer Publishing, Ltd., 1996.

Cecil, Victoria. *Minton 'Majolica.' An Historical Survey and Exhibition Catalogue.* London: Jeremy Cooper Ltd., 1982.

The Centennial Exposition Guide 1876, Fairmount Park. Philadelphia, Pennsylvania: Hamlin & Lawrence, 1876.

Clegg, Miriam (ed.). "The Phoenix Pottery." *Historical Society of the Phoenixville Area* 8(2), December 1984.

Cluett, Robert. *George Jones Ceramics 1861-1951.* Atglen, Pennsylvania: Schiffer Publishing, Ltd., 1998.

Congdon-Martin, Douglas. *America For Sale. A Collector's Guide to Antique Advertising.* Atglen, Pennsylvania: Schiffer Publishing, Ltd., 1991.

Cunningham, Helen. *Majolica Figures.* Atglen, Pennsylvania: Schiffer Publishing, Ltd., 1997.

Cushion, John P. *Animals in Pottery and Porcelain.* New York: Crown Publishers, Inc., 1974.

Cushion, John P. and William B. Honey. *Handbook of Pottery & Porcelain Marks.* 4th ed. London: Faber & Faber, 1980.

Dawes, Nicholas M. *Majolica.* New York: Crown Publishers, Inc., 1990.

Erardi, Glenn and Pauline C. Peck. *Mustache Cups. Timeless Victorian Treasures.* Atglen, Pennsylvania: Schiffer Publishing, Ltd., 1999.

Ewins, Neil. "Supplying the Present Wants of Our Yankee Cousins ...: Staffordshire Ceramics and the American Market 1775-1880." *Journal of Ceramic History* 15, 1997.

Godden, Geoffrey A. *Encyclopaedia of British Pottery and Porcelain Marks.* New York: Bonanza Books, 1964.

_____. *The Concise Guide to British Pottery and Porcelain.* London: Barrie & Jenkins, 1990.

Halfpenny, Pat. *English Earthenware Figures: 1740-1840.* Woodbridge, Suffolk: Antiques Collectors' Club, 1991.

Hall, John. *Staffordshire Pottery Figures.* New York: The World Publishing Company, 1972.

Horowitz, Joe. *Figural Tobacco Jars: An Introduction and Illustrated Guide to Values.* Baltimore, Maryland: FTJ Publishing, 1994.

Jewitt, Llewellynn. *The Ceramic Art of Great Britain.* London: J.S. Virtue and Company, 1878; rev. 1883.

Jones, Joan. *Minton: The First Two Hundred Years of Design and Production.* Shrewsbury, England: Swan Hill Press, 1993.

Karmason, Marilyn G. with Joan B. Stacke. *Majolica. A Complete History and Illustrated Survey.* New York: Harry N. Abrams, 1989.

Karsnitz, Jim and Vivian. *Oyster Plates.* Atglen, Pennsylvania: Schiffer Publishing, Ltd., 1993.

Katz-Marks, Mariann. *The Collector's Encyclopedia of Majolica: An Identification and Value Guide.* Paducah, Kentucky: Collector Books, 1992.

Kowalsky, Arnold A. and Dorothy E. *Encyclopedia of Marks on American, English, and European Earthenware, Ironstone, and Stoneware.* Atglen, Pennsylvania: Schiffer Publishing, Ltd., 1999.

Lehner, Lois. *Lehner's Encyclopedia of U.S. Marks on Pottery, Porcelain, and Clay.* Paducah, Kentucky: Collector Books, 1988.

Moore, N. Hudson. *The Old China Book including Staffordshire, Wedgwood, Lustre and Other English Pottery and Porcelain.* New York: Tudor Publishing Company, 1903.

Murray, D. Michael. *European Majolica.* Atglen, Pennsylvania: Schiffer Publishing, Ltd., 1997.

Official Catalogue of the Great Exhibition of the Works of Industry of All Nations, 1851. By Authority of the Royal Commission. London: W. Clowes & Sons, Printers, 1852.

Quillman, Catherine. "Phoenixville firm known for majolica pottery." *Philadephia Inquirer,* Chester County Home Page B2, August 28, 2000.

Rebert, M. Charles. *American Majolica: 1850-1900.* Des Moines, Iowa: Wallace-Homestead Book Company, 1981.

Reports by the Juries on the Subject in the Thirty Classes into Which the Exhibition Was Divided. By Authority of the Royal Commission. London: W. Clowes & Sons, Printers, 1852.

Röntgen, Robert E. *Marks on German, Bohemian and Austrian Porcelain: 1710 to the Present.* Atglen, Pennsylvania: Schiffer Publishing, Ltd., 1981.

Rydell, Robert W. *All the World's a Fair. Visions of Empire at American International Expositions, 1876-1916.* Chicago, Illinois: The University of Chicago Press, 1984.

Savage, George and Harold Newman. *An Illustrated Dictionary of Ceramics.* London: Thames and Hudson Ltd., 1974.

Schneider, Mike. *Majolica.* Atglen, Pennsylvania: Schiffer Publishing, Ltd., 1990.

Snyder, Jeffrey B. "American majolica dazzled fair goers in 1876." *Antique Week* 33(10), May 22, 2000.

Snyder, Jeffrey B. and Leslie Bockol. *Majolica: American & European Wares.* Atglen, Pennsylvania: Schiffer Publishing, Ltd., 1994.

Stern, Anne M.P. "Colorful Majolica." *Majolica Matters*, Summer 1992.

Weidner, Brooke. *Catalogue of Majolica 1884.* Phoenixville, Pennsylvania: Brooke Weidner, 1960 (reprint of the 1884 Griffen, Smith & Company World's Industrial and Cotton Centennial Exposition catalog).

Williams, Peter. *Wedgwood: A Collector's Guide.* Radnor, Pennsylvania: Wallace-Homestead Book Company, 1992.

Williams, Susan. *Savory Suppers and Fashionable Feasts. Dining in Victorian America.* New York: Pantheon Books, 1985.

Yarnell, Druscilla Smith. "Penned history of her father's (David Smith) association with a local pottery which produced majolica: Griffen, Smith & Hill." *Historical Society of the Phoenixville Area*, n.d.

Index